2021

CHRISTMAS

with

Southern Living.

2021

CHRISTMAS

with

Southern Living

INSPIRED IDEAS FOR HOLIDAY COOKING & DECORATING

Southern Living **BOOKS**

Conte

nts

Simple and stately, wreaths of evergreen and Southern magnolia accented with red velvet bows grace the windows, lamppost, and mailbox (page 2) of this home that is dressed for the festive season.

That wonderful time of year, full of expectation & joy, is upon us.

After shutdowns, distance, and virtual gatherings, the best gift of all is being able to gather more safely again. It sure feels like something to sing about, and this year's decorating section happens to be inspired by songs, such as Elvis Presley's "Blue Christmas," Dolly Parton's "Shine On," and the classic carols "Merry Little Christmas" and "Winter Wonderland."

We produced this edition during the winter of 2020, amid the pandemic, with a tiny team and lots of outdoor photography so that we could be safe while creating lots of Christmas cheer for readers. The setting for the Decorate chapter was the small historic community of the Monteagle Sunday School Assembly (MSSA) in the Tennessee mountains near the University of the South at Sewanee. Sometimes referred to as "The Chautauqua of the South," the community was chartered in 1882 and patterned after the Chautauqua Institution in New York with the purpose of "the advancement of science, literary attainment, Sunday School interests, and the promotion of the broadest popular culture in the interest of Christianity without regard to sect or denomination."

In 1982, the MSSA was placed in the National Register of Historic Places by the U.S. Department of the Interior. The community is home to over 160 picturesque Victorian and early 20th-Century cottages on a campus of 354 acres. Most are second homes enjoyed as an escape for families during the hot summer months. We practically had the place to ourselves and found beauty around every corner in the architecture, mature forest of soaring pine, cypress, and magnolia, and the sounds of nature uninterrupted by people. Our time there felt as if we had ventured into the past and we appreciated every lovely minute of getting to be creative in such an uncommonly beautiful place. I hope you like what you see!

I also hope that the menus and recipes found in the Entertain and Savor & Share sections inspire you to cook together, eat together, and linger together at the table once again. Let this book be your guide to making every minute of this holiday memorable. Be sure to use the Holiday Planner in the back of the book to get organized and to jot down ideas and reflections along the way.

Here's to you and yours this holiday!

Katherine Cobbs

EDITOR, *SOUTHERN LIVING* BOOKS

Deco

HOLIDAY LOOKBOOK

rate

BLUE CHRISTMAS

Elvis' popular holiday tune serves as a jumping-off point for an outdoor holiday display. Various shades of blue woven with copper, rusted metal, native stone, warm wood tones, and lots of texture create a timeless look that's as comforting as a favorite pair of jeans...or blue suede shoes.

OPPOSITE: A cabin recently designed by Alabama architect James Carter only looks as if it's been nestled in the woods for generations. Its board-and-chinking siding is a fitting backdrop for woodland-inspired decorations. Mixed boughs of silvery-blue Carolina Sapphire Cypress and pine are woven into a garland accented with pine cones, eryngium, magnolia leaves, and vintage blue Christmas lights. Dried sponge mushrooms and icy eucalyptus add interest to the wreath gracing the door. **THIS PAGE:** A tiered copper stand does double-duty as a workstation for decking the outdoors, as well as a spot for gathering gifts for guests or hosts.

So Delightful

A roaring fire, cozy wool blankets, hot drinks, and roasting chestnuts (see page 183 for the roasting how-to) keep the fun outside beneath the stars after an afternoon spent sprucing up the exterior for the festive season ahead. A fresh-cut cypress tree is a lovely, lacy Southern native with an ideal form for decorating.

Hit the Right Notes

Sticking to the Blue Christmas theme is simple when relying on foraged finds from the surrounding forest—dark evergreens and blue-green conifer boughs play well with lichen-crusted branches, pine cones, and the coppery velvet backsides of Southern magnolia leaves. It's a rich palette repeated in the ribbons, wreaths, and antique copper chestnut roaster. On the side of a garden shed crafted from antique barn boards, a wrought-iron planter corrals fresh cuttings ready to be incorporated into wreaths, garlands, and swags.

Make It Sing!

Start with a harmonious color scheme. Across the color wheel from blue is orange, which is considered its complementary color cousin. Elements with rusty undertones are warm sidekicks that pair beautifully with a range of cool blues. We started the inspiration board for this cabin's décor with a nod to the natural surroundings. A mix of fresh clippings and florist finds, including dried botanical elements, keeps things interesting. Burlap and kraft paper lend organic textures that help all the other accents shine. An iron bird feeder, sea glass beads, vintage bulbs, and shimmering mercury glass acorn ornaments set the tone for this rustic approach.

Serenade of
NATURE

—

Get inspiration for gift-giving from your décor or vice versa. If you love gardening, the outdoors, or are decorating with elements from your surroundings, consider giving gifts with a similar natural sensibility. Stick to the same color palette so that you can incorporate the same ribbon and decorative elements from your décor onto wrapped packages. Whether you wrap one small surprise to tuck into a stocking or choose to fill a basket to its brim, make it special. Satin ribbon and a tiny garden-tool ornament give a kraft paper package high-low style. Combining lots of small gifts in one large container wows—it's a gift that keeps on giving.

Think Inside the Box!

A vintage metal picnic tin with bamboo handles and a painted, woven-wicker design doesn't need much embellishment. Line the bottom with balls of recycled paper topped with a few layers of pretty tissue and shredded paper to create nests for arranging items at varying heights in the box. Sticking with an indigo-accented nature theme, we compiled gifts for the gardener, including a carved mushroom-shaped birdhouse, a miniature bluebird figurine, a stocking ornament coated in birdseed, denim-and-leather gardening gloves, copper plant markers, seed packets with a custom stamp for saving and sharing seeds, hand salve, a nail brush, lip balm, and scented soap. Any one of these surprises makes a great gift on its own, but together they make a bold statement.

SHINE ON

Dolly Parton's soulful song "Shine On" was written to Tammy Wynette in memoriam, but the powerful lyrics about the gift of love divine are especially fitting for Christmas. Both the song and country music icon inspire the shimmery, glimmery, feminine approach to dressing up this pretty little jewel box of a Victorian cottage in the Tennessee mountains for the holidays.

OPPOSITE: A frilly cypress garland and swag of gray-washed wooden beads frames the double screen doors of this stately mountain cottage accented with gingerbread architectural details. A wicker chair is the perfect porch perch for greeting passersby, collecting packages, or taking in the magic of a Christmas tree planted in a blush pink pedestal planter. **THIS PAGE:** Natural and bleached pampas grasses give feathery texture to simple evergreen wreaths embellished with shimmering dried lunaria and organza ribbon. Blushing berries dress up the garland-draped porch railing.

Most Wonderful Time

A neoclassical grandfather clock with gilded ormolu workings gets even more dressed up for a party with a shawl of icicle-draped garland accented with sand roses, amaryllis, and berries. A wall of antique French faience oyster plates conjures wintry wreaths above the candlelit sideboard set for a predinner toast. More sand roses mixed with cream and coral amaryllis, ostrich feathers, lacy leaves, and pink berries create a striking centerpiece.

Hit the Right Notes

Feminine but not fussy, snowy drifts of bleached pampas grass layered over a blanket of mixed conifer boughs soften a stately fireplace made of native stone. A forest of painted mercury glass trees and flickering candles in pink hobnail votives shine on above a roaring fire below. Geometric gray embroidery keeps pink velvet stockings from looking too precious while a warm woven throw for cozying up by the fire repeats the linear pattern. Judicious use of dove and charcoal gray adds doses of handsome to balance all the pretty here.

Make It Sing!

Using Dolly Parton's song "Shine On" for inspiration, decorative elements with a bit of shimmer—quartz, selenite, and pearl—are fitting starting points for this cottage's holiday décor. Less expected natural elements like pampas grass, lunaria, and feathers add fresh fun to complement the rich textures and finishes. Don't be afraid to mix flowers into greenery, wreaths, and garlands. Dark green plastic water tubes that florists use for cut flowers keep the blossoms fresh. Be sure to bring any outdoor floral displays indoors before a freeze. By sticking to botanical elements in subdued shades of cream, beige, champagne, blush, and rose, it's easy to achieve a cohesive look that pops against the rich backdrop of traditional evergreens.

Serenade of
COMFORTS
—

The holidays are tailor-made for gathering and, quite often, that means hosting a house guest...or a few. Taking a cue from the welcoming holiday décor here, a gift box packed with unexpected comforts is a pretty present that any guest would be over the moon to find waiting for them in the guest room. Keep the look simple and cohesive by sticking to the "Shine On" color palette. Simply fill a basket or box with an array of gifts with pampering in mind. Keep the look pretty or style things with a more masculine sensibility. The key takeaway is to shower your houseguests with those little things that provide added comfort during their stay, or are items that they may have forgotten to pack.

Think Inside the Box!

A heavy cardboard gift box in a gray and white faux bois print is a wintry package that is ideal for nestling lots of comforting surprises: a floral posey for the bedside table, tapers and votives with matches for lighting, scented lotion, French-milled soaps, calming bath salts, a tin of tea with a lovely little strainer, and pretty note cards for writing thank-you notes. These are small gifts on their own that when combined make a big impression that guests will appreciate. Change things up by including cozy socks, shaving cream, a cocktail kit, a favorite novel, a satin sleep mask, or whatever may fit the recipient's style and sensibilities.

MERRY LITTLE CHRISTMAS

It's hard not to have yourself a merry little Christmas when surrounded by whimsical décor in a traditional holiday color scheme with lots of sweet surprises at every turn. Although the classic Christmas carol that inspired this look is a tad melancholy, the decked-out halls of this rustic cabin in the woods radiate joy and good cheer.

OPPOSITE: The outdoors are reflected in a patinated pine mirror draped with a trio of boxwood wreaths, bringing shimmering light into the entry. A painted green antique chest corrals caramel apple party favors and features a playful North Pole take on a nativity scene, while a simple laser-cut tree with swiveling branches adds height and a woodsy touch to the corner. **THIS PAGE:** Holiday cards displayed on a mirror's frame transform the mudroom from a pass-through to a place to linger to straighten hats and scarves while taking in the news from family and friends near and far.

Making Spirits Bright

Candy becomes décor (at least as long as it lasts) in an easy-to-set-up hot cocoa station. This is a striking way to entice young and old to gather together and create something delicious to sip while sharing stories by the fire. An old bottle-drying rack holds cups brimming with candy. Vintage milk glass mugs and an apothecary jar keep more sweet treats at the ready for embellishing drinks to suit tastes.

OPPOSITE: A map of Tennessee's Cumberland Plateau is a nod to place and a striking focal point in red and green above a mantel lined with boxwood and berries. A hand-forged iron sconce gets softened with a woven bow and ring of more boxwood. Chunky fisherman's knit stockings can hold almost as much as Santa's sack. **THIS PAGE:** In the bunkroom, a metal herb-drying rack becomes an Advent calendar mobile hung with tiny gifts to open each evening at bedtime.

Hit the Right Notes

The joy of little ones at Christmastime is infectious, and the décor for this mountain vacation home is all about the magic and whimsy of the season with a nod to the traditional. Classic colors are an obvious choice that plays well against the white shiplap and board-and-chinking backdrops of the cabin's walls. Candy confections become the main decorative elements here. Bonus: Much will get eaten so there will be less to put away after the holidays.

Make It Sing!

A mix of preserved and fresh boxwood accented with faux red berries keeps the wreaths and garlands streamlined, simple, and very merry. Pops of more red and green come from a candy store-size stash of vintage sweets, which are also used as drink stirrers, gift toppers, and Advent calendar surprises. Swap in tiny ornaments and non-edible accents in red and green for a sugar-free spin that can be just as merry only without the crash.

Think Inside the Box!

A wicker basket with a handle is very Little Red Riding Hood, but these goodies aren't just reserved for grandma. After all, it's a most wonderful time of year for sharing so we packed this gift basket with lots of sweet surprises and nostalgic candy favorites that will entice young and old alike. Organza sacks, cellophane gift bags tied with twine, and paper cupcake liners keep things separated. Extras like Christmas cookie cutters, a canister of hot cocoa mix, a jar of caramel sauce with shiny red apples for dipping, and a vintage-style ornament or two are things to enjoy now and in the weeks to come.

Serenade of SWEETS

Whether it's rolling out the dough for Christmas cookie cutouts or making a cream-filled yule log for the holiday dessert table, Christmas would be less merry without a few sweet indulgences. Create a basket of confections that will wow your recipient and match his or her sweet tooth. Is your colleague a chocolate addict? Follow that decadent direction. Does your daughter love macarons? Pile them up in shades of red, white, and green. Stick to classic Southern candies like Ruth Hunt Candies, Chick-O-Sticks, and Peanut Patties, to name a few, or tuck in festive things like a hot cocoa mug, ornament, or snow globe.

WINTER WONDERLAND

Sleighbells and snowmen are the stuff of the classic holiday carol that inspires the decorating theme here, only we bring them inside beneath glass to create enchanted snowy worlds that Southerners only sometimes get to see outside their windows. Doses of scarlet pop against a palette of snow white, black, antique gold, and raw wood in this home with something to draw you in around every corner.

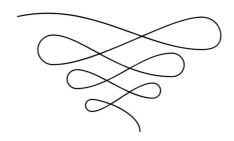

OPPOSITE: Don't overlook the opportunity that decorating the inside of the front door offers. Blossoms like these striking scarlet anemones and stunning red and white amaryllis would freeze outdoors if the mercury plunges but will last for weeks indoors. **THIS PAGE:** Faux snow dusts the bottom of a terrarium holding a potted white orchid displayed on a chest with brass deer, greenery, and flickering votives in the foyer. A simple swag of greenery accents one corner of the antique mirror that reflects the chandelier beyond.

Mini Marvels

Glass cloches top enchanted scenes created with live and faux plants and miniature accents arranged on frosty plates, cake stands, and mirrors along the expanse of a console table in the living room.

MERRY
CHRISTMAS

Hit the Right Notes

OPPOSITE: A feathery mane of cypress and boxwood surrounds antlers mounted on a plaque with more woven through the collection of antlers in a bowl beneath. Glass house ornaments filled with tiny surprises hang from the horns to create a striking focal point in this cozy den. **THIS PAGE:** Cake domes and garden cloches take the snow globe to a more substantial level and can accommodate miniatures, plants, and festive figurines. Evergreen sprigs, balls of moss, and red berries add pizzazz beneath pillar candles in lanterns on the hearth.

Table Magic

An over-the-top, lush display of vibrant red anemones with rich black centers and creamy Lenten roses beckons diners to the table while playing off the mismatched, black-and-white table settings. The key to making this centerpiece last through multiple meals is well-soaked floral foam on top of plastic sheeting to protect the table. The abundant blossoms and lacy cypress boughs camouflage the plastic.

Make It Sing!

Taking inventory of the decorative pieces already in the home—glass vases, lanterns, cake domes, and terrarium—inspired these winter wonderlands behind glass. Faux snow is an obvious accent, as are vintage ornaments, package toppers, and small toys. Figurative approaches for some displays and all-natural elements in others keep the décor from looking too precious. When creating a terrarium with live plants, look for packets of faux snow that you mix with water so it multiplies in volume. It looks so real and the moisture keeps plants hydrated. Mist as needed from time to time to rehydrate the snow. After the holidays, the faux snow can be added to the soil of houseplants and outdoor planters to keep the plants from drying out too quickly.

Happy Holidays

Serenade of
WONDER
___

During this season of wonder, it makes sense to give gifts that inspire creativity and awe all year long. The enchantment of the mini winter wonderlands created for the holidays here can last well after the last ornament is packed. Terrarium gifts are easy on the budget and so simple to put together. Creating and maintaining a terrarium is a low-maintenance enterprise with a satisfying payoff: watching it grow! There are two types of terrariums: open and sealed. Open ones are the most versatile. They have lids that allow fresh air, water, and new plants and accents to be added. They're the easiest to maintain even if you don't have a green thumb. Be sure to select plants with similar light and watering needs. Don't put a cactus with a fern or a succulent with a mini palm tree and expect great results.

Think Inside the Box!

Using an inexpensive wooden planter lined with handmade paper as a gift box is a fitting package for a mini garden. To make a terrarium kit, package up a soil-less potting mix, coarse sand, pea gravel, ball moss, and faux snow in cellophane bags tied with ribbon or twine. Add a few helpful tools like a mister and mini rake, as well as a few decorative accents to help personalize the gift. Small, slow-growing plants with similar light and water requirements are key to success. Include a small terrarium, vase, or jar with a manageable-size opening, as the ecosystem for your enchanted garden gift.

Enter

HOLIDAY MENUS

tain

FAR-FLUNG FRIENDSGIVING

Even if a journey from kitchen to dining room is the only one on the itinerary, our tastebuds can transport us to faraway places. This menu is all about incorporating exotic flavors into classic Thanksgiving standards for a festive and fun new take on tradition.

MENU
—

Lychee Martinis

Rumaki Skewers

Hoisin Duck

Five-Spice Cranberry Sauce

Ginger-Sesame Sweet Potato Soufflé

Long Bean & Shiitake Saute

Cloverleaf Sichuan-Scallion Buns

Coco-Peanut Chess Pie

Lychee Martini

Lychee fruit are available fresh or peeled and canned in syrup. This cocktail calls for the latter so that you have the syrup from the can to use as a mixer. Garnish with canned lychee or a peeled, fresh one. The flavor of the fruit has floral and pear notes that work well in this unique made-to-order fall tipple.

SERVES **1**   ACTIVE **5 MIN.**   TOTAL **5 MIN.**

- ⅓ cup (3 oz.) Bartlett pear vodka (such as Skyy brand)
- 2 tablespoons (1 oz.) dry vermouth
- ¼ cup (2 oz.) syrup from canned lychee
- Lychee fruit
- Seckel pear or Bartlett pear slice

Combine the vodka, vermouth, and lychee syrup in a cocktail shaker with ice. Shake vigorously. Strain into a chilled martini glass. Garnish with a lychee fruit and pear slice.

Make It a Mocktail!

Substitute 2 oz. unsweetened pear nectar and 2 oz. spring water for the vodka and vermouth for a non-alcoholic drink.

ENTERTAIN

Rumaki Skewers

This recipe is a deconstructed spin on rumaki, a mid-century cocktail hour nibble that swaps water chestnuts for the chicken livers and sausage for the smoky shawl of bacon. This is a guaranteed crowd-pleaser.

SERVES **8 TO 10**   ACTIVE **20 MIN.**   TOTAL **40 MIN.**

- 24 (½-in.) slices cooked smoked sausage (such as Conecuh brand)
- 2 (8-oz.) cans whole water chestnuts, drained and rinsed
- ¼ cup soy sauce
- 1½ Tbsp. balsamic vinegar
- 2 tsp. honey
- 1 Tbsp. lime zest
- 2 Tbsp. minced fresh ginger
- ½ tsp. crushed red pepper
- 2 scallions, sliced (about ¼ cup)

1. Preheat oven to 375°F. Thread 24 short cocktail skewers with 1 sausage slice and 1 whole water chestnut (reserve leftover water chestnuts for another use).

2. Combine the soy sauce, vinegar, honey, lime zest, ginger, and crushed red pepper in a bowl, whisking until honey dissolves. Brush skewers with glaze; arrange on a rack set on a baking sheet lined with aluminum foil.

3. Bake in preheated oven until the sausage is hot and the sauce begins to caramelize, 18 to 20 minutes. Transfer skewers to a serving platter and sprinkle with sliced scallions.

JUMPSTART!

Thread the skewers and make the glaze a day (or two) before Thanksgiving. Bring both to room temperature while the oven preheats.

Hoisin Duck

The secret to crispy skin is to dry the exterior of the duck thoroughly with paper towels before, during, and after refrigerating. Store the birds uncovered in the back, coldest part of your fridge for up to two days to let them air-dry thoroughly before seasoning to roast.

SERVES **8 TO 10**   ACTIVE **30 MIN.**
TOTAL **11 HOURS, 50 MIN.**

—

2 (6- to 7-lb.) whole ducks

Kitchen string

2 tsp. kosher salt

½ tsp. freshly ground black pepper

⅓ cup hoisin sauce

¼ cup orange juice

2 Tbsp. honey

2 Tbsp. fresh lemon juice (from 1 lemon)

1 tsp. chili oil

1. Remove giblets from ducks and reserve for another use. Rinse ducks, and pat dry with paper towels. Remove excess fat and skin. Tie legs together with kitchen string; chill, uncovered, 10 to 24 hours.

2. Preheat oven to 450°F. Let ducks stand at room temperature 15 minutes. Prick legs, thighs, and breasts with a fork. Rub ducks with salt and black pepper, and place, breast side up, on a wire rack in an aluminum foil-lined jelly-roll pan. Bake 45 minutes.

3. Meanwhile, stir together hoisin sauce and next 4 ingredients in a small bowl. Remove ducks from oven, and carefully spoon fat from pan. Brush ducks with half the hoisin glaze. Reduce oven temperature to 350°F. Bake 15 minutes; baste with remaining glaze and bake 10 to 15 minutes more or until a meat thermometer inserted in thickest portion registers 180°F. Let stand 15 minutes before serving.

TEST KITCHEN TIP: When roasting duck, pricking the skin before it goes into the oven allows the fat beneath it to escape as it renders in the heat of the oven. It is important to thoroughly dry the bird inside and out to reduce spattering; season it with salt and black pepper, and place the bird on a rack breast side down, uncovered, in the refrigerator overnight. These steps allow the skin to dry out completely, which helps it crisp as it roasts.

Five-Spice Cranberry Sauce

Tinged with the exotic warm notes of clove, cinnamon, star anise, fennel, and Sichuan peppercorns, the shortcut to flavor in this tangy cranberry sauce comes from a jar of Chinese five-spice powder. It's a great addition to your kitchen cupboard. Use it in rubs for meat before grilling, add it to chicken salad, or dust the top of a bowl of chicken soup with a dash or two for a flavor boost.

SERVES **12**   ACTIVE **20 MIN.**   TOTAL **2 HOURS, 30 MIN.**

—

1 (12-oz.) pkg. fresh or frozen whole cranberries

1 shallot, thinly sliced (¼ cup)

¼ cup packed brown sugar

1 Tbsp. honey

¼ tsp. kosher salt

¼ tsp. teaspoon Chinese five-spice powder

2 tsp. orange zest plus ¼ cup fresh orange juice (from 1 navel orange), divided

Combine cranberries, shallot, brown sugar, honey, salt, five-spice powder, and orange juice in a medium saucepan over medium-high, and cook, stirring occasionally, until cranberries burst and liquid starts to reduce, about 15 minutes. Reduce heat to low, and simmer until liquid has a thick, syrupy consistency, about 12 minutes. Remove from heat, and cool completely, about 2 hours. (Sauce will continue to thicken as it cools.) Sprinkle with orange zest.

Tasty Swap

Try this cranberry sauce with other spice blends like pumpkin pie spice, mulling spice, or even chai spice for three new takes on this recipe.

ENTERTAIN

Ginger-Sesame Sweet Potato Soufflé

A sesame streusel topping takes the place of the usual nutty crumble on this flavorful soufflé.

SERVES **8**   ACTIVE **15 MIN.**   TOTAL **1 HOUR, 15 MIN.**

½ cup (4 oz.) unsalted butter, softened, divided

2 large eggs, lightly beaten

3½ cups mashed cooked sweet potatoes

½ cup heavy cream

2 tsp. kosher salt

1 tsp. toasted sesame oil

½ tsp. pumpkin pie spice

1 cup packed light brown sugar, divided

¼ cup all-purpose flour

¼ cup sesame seeds

1. Preheat oven to 375°F. Coat a 1-quart round soufflé dish with 1 tablespoon of the butter. Microwave remaining 7 tablespoons butter in a small microwavable bowl on HIGH until melted, about 30 seconds. Let cool 3 minutes.

2. Stir together eggs, sweet potatoes, cream, salt, sesame oil, pumpkin pie spice, ¾ cup of the brown sugar, and 4 tablespoons of the melted butter in a large bowl until completely smooth. Pour batter into prepared soufflé dish; bake at 375°F until beginning to set, about 30 minutes.

3. Meanwhile, stir together flour, sesame seeds, and remaining ¼ cup brown sugar and 3 tablespoons softened butter in a bowl until just combined.

4. Remove soufflé from oven; top evenly with sesame-flour mixture. Return to oven; bake in preheated oven until golden brown, about 30 minutes. Let cool slightly, about 10 minutes. Serve warm.

Long Bean & Shiitake Saute

Look for long beans at Asian markets or substitute regular green beans here.

SERVES **8**   ACTIVE **15 MIN.**   TOTAL **15 MIN.**

3 Tbsp. vegetable oil, divided

2 lb. long beans, trimmed and cut into 3-in. lengths

½ cup sliced cremini mushrooms

½ cup sliced shiitake mushrooms

2 Tbsp. butter

3 Tbsp. minced shallot

2 garlic cloves, chopped

2 Tbsp. dry sherry

2 Tbsp. soy sauce

1 Tbsp. Asian chili garlic sauce

1. Heat a large skillet over medium-high. Add 1 tablespoon oil; swirl to coat. Add beans; cook, stirring frequently, until blistered and mostly tender, about 6 minutes. Transfer to a bowl.

2. Heat remaining oil over high. Add mushrooms in a single layer. Cook 4 to 6 minutes or until golden and browned. Transfer to bowl with beans.

3. Melt butter in skillet over medium-high. Add shallots and garlic and cook 2 minutes, stirring frequently. Stir in sherry, soy sauce, and chili garlic sauce and bring to a boil. Return mushrooms and beans to skillet and cook, stirring often, until hot and coated with sauce. Serve warm.

Cloverleaf Sichuan-Scallion Buns

Savory, tender, and accented with red sichuan pepper and green scallions, these delicious rolls would also be a festive addition to a Christmas menu.

MAKES **12**   ACTIVE **25 MIN.**   TOTAL **2 HOURS, 15 MIN.**

1 cup warm milk (100°F to 110°F)

1 (¼-oz.) envelope active dry yeast

2 Tbsp. granulated sugar, divided

3 cups (about 12¾ oz.) all-purpose flour

1¼ tsp. flaky sea salt

6 Tbsp. butter, melted

1 large egg, lightly beaten

1½ tsp. ground Sichuan peppercorns

1 Tbsp. chopped scallion

1. Stir together milk, yeast, and 1 tablespoon of the sugar in a 2-cup glass measuring cup; let stand 5 minutes.

2. Combine flour, sea salt, and remaining 1 tablespoon sugar in bowl of a heavy-duty electric stand mixer; let stand 5 minutes. Add 4 tablespoons of the melted butter, egg, and yeast mixture; beat at low speed, using paddle attachment, 3 minutes or until blended and a soft, sticky dough forms. Increase speed to medium, attach dough hook and beat 6 minutes or until dough is smooth and elastic but still slightly sticky. Cover bowl with plastic wrap, and let rise in a warm place (85°F), free from drafts, 1 hour or until doubled in bulk.

3. Punch dough down. Turn out onto a lightly floured surface. Divide dough into 12 equal portions (about 2 ounces each). Gently shape each portion into 3 (1¼-inch) balls; place in 12 buttered muffin cups. Brush tops of dough with remaining 2 tablespoons melted butter. Cover and let rise in a warm (85°F) place, free from drafts, 30 to 45 minutes or until doubled in bulk.

4. Preheat oven to 375°F. Sprinkle rolls with Sichuan pepper and chopped scallions.

5. Bake in preheated oven until golden brown, 15 to 17 minutes. Transfer to a wire rack. Serve warm, or cool completely (about 30 minutes).

Tasty Swap

These yeasty rolls are a savory backdrop for other tasty toppings. Substitute crushed red pepper and chives, or cracked black pepper and chopped fresh herbs, such as rosemary, thyme, or oregano for the Sichuan pepper and scallions here.

ENTERTAIN

Coco-Peanut Chess Pie

The added salinity from salt-roasted peanuts amps up the flavors of this lusciously sublime swap for traditional pecan pie.

SERVES **8**   ACTIVE **18 MIN.**   TOTAL **1 HOUR, 18 MIN.**

½ (14.1-oz.) pkg. refrigerated piecrusts

2 cups granulated sugar

2 Tbsp. cornmeal

1 Tbsp. all-purpose flour

¼ tsp. table salt

½ cup butter, melted

½ cup creamy peanut butter

1 Tbsp. white vinegar

1 tsp. vanilla extract

4 large eggs, lightly beaten

1 cup toasted flaked coconut, plus more for garnish

Sweetened whipped cream

Chopped peanuts

1. Preheat oven to 350°F. Fit piecrust into a 9-inch pie plate according to package directions; fold edges under, and crimp. Prick bottom of crust all over with a fork.

2. Place pie pan in the freezer for dough to chill 15 minutes.

3. Stir together 2 cups sugar and next 7 ingredients until blended. Add eggs and coconut, stirring well. Pour into chilled piecrust.

4. Bake in preheated oven 40 to 45 minutes, shielding edges with aluminum foil after 10 minutes to prevent excessive browning. Cool completely on a wire rack. Garnish with whipped cream, chopped peanuts, and toasted flaked coconut before serving.

Tasty Swap

This pie is equally delicious made with cashew butter and chopped cashews or almond butter and chopped slivered almonds.

FARMHOUSE KITCHEN BREAKFAST

Waking up to the aroma of coffee and warm biscuits wafting through the house is enough to rouse most from sweet slumber. Treat your crowd to this stick-to-their-ribs breakfast that will keep them fortified as they deck the halls, shop 'til they drop, or open the gifts beneath the tree.

MENU

—

Tequila Sunrise Spritzers

Honey-Buttermilk Biscuits

Goat Cheese Grits

Country-Fried Steak with Cream Gravy & Fried Eggs

Sunshine Fruit Salad

Cherry-Pie Spice Coffee Cake

Pecan Praline Lattes

Tequila Sunrise Spritzers

Trade in the usual brunch mimosa for this sunny sipper full of juicy flavor.

SERVES **10**   ACTIVE **5 MIN.**   TOTAL **5 MIN.**

2 cups (16 oz.) freshly squeezed orange juice (about 8 oranges), plus orange slices for garnish

2 cups (16 oz.) pineapple juice

2 cups (16 oz.) blanco tequila

1 cup (8 oz.) cranberry juice cocktail

2 Tbsp. (1 oz.) grenadine

Club soda

Maraschino cherries

Combine the first 5 ingredients in a large pitcher. Stir to combine. Pour into tall ice-filled glasses. Top off with club soda. Garnish glasses with cherries and orange slices.

Make It a Mocktail!

Use 2¾ cups each of the orange and pineapple juices and 1½ cups of the cranberry juice cocktail to replace the tequila for a non-alcoholic spritzer.

Honey-Buttermilk Biscuits

This super simple recipe comes together fast—no rolling or cutting required! Enjoy the hot biscuits with butter and honey or smother them in rich Cream Gravy (page 83).

MAKES **14**   ACTIVE **15 MIN.**   TOTAL **25 MIN.**

2½ cups (about 10 oz.) self-rising flour

1¼ cups chilled buttermilk

1 tsp. honey

½ cup, plus 2 Tbsp. butter, melted and divided

Parchment paper

1. Preheat oven to 475°F. Sift flour in a large bowl.

2. Stir together buttermilk, honey, and ½ cup melted butter in a small bowl. (Butter will clump.) Stir buttermilk mixture into flour mixture until dough pulls away from sides of bowl. Drop dough by level scoops, 1 inch apart, onto a parchment paper-lined baking pan. (Use a 2-inch cookie scoop.)

3. Bake in preheated oven 12 minutes or until golden brown. Brush with 2 tablespoons melted butter, and serve.

Goat Cheese Grits

Quick-cooking grits cook in a mere five minutes and are a hearty alternative to oatmeal for breakfast.

SERVES **8**   ACTIVE **10 MIN.**   TOTAL **30 MIN.**

9 cups low-sodium chicken broth

3 cups uncooked quick-cooking grits

8 oz. soft goat cheese, crumbled (about 2 cups)

8 scallions, white and light green parts only, chopped (about 1 cup)

Table salt

Chopped fresh flat-leaf parsley

Crushed red pepper

In a medium saucepan, bring chicken broth to a boil over high heat. Gradually whisk in grits, reduce heat to low and cook, whisking, until very thick, approximately 4½ minutes. Whisk in cheese and scallions until well combined. Taste and season with salt, if desired. Remove from heat and cover to keep warm. Top with parsley and crushed red pepper to serve.

TEST KITCHEN TIP: If you don't have quick-cooking grits in your pantry, this recipe can be made with regular or stone-ground grits cooked in chicken broth for the amount of time noted on the package directions. Simply whisk in the add-ins as soon as the grits have cooked through.

Country-Fried Steaks with Cream Gravy & Fried Eggs

This hearty breakfast is a holiday treat. Fry the eggs and make the gravy first and keep them warm while you prepare the steaks. Garnishing the gravy with chopped fresh parsley and a sprinkling of freshly ground pink peppercorns adds holiday flair.

SERVES **6**   ACTIVE **35 MIN.**
TOTAL **1 HOUR, 25 MIN., INCLUDING GRAVY**

---

6 (6-oz.) top sirloin steaks, cubed

1 tsp. kosher salt

¼ tsp. black pepper

3 cups (about 12¾ oz. all-purpose flour

1½ cups finely crushed round buttery crackers

6 Tbsp. chopped fresh oregano

3 large eggs

2 cups buttermilk

Vegetable oil

6 fried eggs

Chopped fresh flat-leaf parsley

Cream Gravy (recipe follows)

1. Sprinkle cubed steaks with salt and black pepper. Combine flour, crackers, and oregano in a shallow dish. Whisk 3 eggs and buttermilk in a bowl.

2. Dip steaks in egg mixture; dredge in cracker mixture. Repeat procedure.

3. Pour oil to depth of 1½ inches in a large heavy skillet. Heat to 325°F. Fry steaks, in batches, 5 to 7 minutes on each side or until golden brown. Drain on a wire rack in a jelly-roll pan. Divide steaks among plates and top with fried eggs and chopped fresh parsley. Serve with gravy.

Cream Gravy

¼ cup flour

1 tsp. kosher salt

1 tsp. black pepper

2 tsp. bacon drippings

2 cups milk

2 cups buttermilk

Ground pink peppercorns

Whisk together the flour, salt, and black pepper. Heat a large skillet with the bacon drippings over medium. Whisk the flour mixture into reserved drippings in skillet; reduce the heat to low and cook 3 minutes, stirring occasionally. Slowly add the milk and buttermilk, whisking constantly. Cook over medium-high, stirring often, 10 to 12 minutes or until thickened. Spoon over country-fried steaks and garnish with the parsley and pink pepper. MAKES ABOUT 3⅔ CUPS

TEST KITCHEN TIP: Traditionally, buttermilk was the liquid drained from churned butter, but today it is made by adding special bacteria to nonfat or low-fat milk; it has a tangy flavor and a creamy texture. If you do not have buttermilk on hand, an easy cheat is to stir 1 tablespoon freshly squeezed lemon juice into 1 cup of milk to replace each cup of buttermilk called for in your recipe.

How to Release the Seeds from a Pomegranate

You can buy pomegranate seeds, or arils, in containers in the produce section, but seeding a pomegranate isn't difficult and doesn't have to stain your fingers or counters. Arils keep in the fridge for 2 weeks and the freezer for several months.

1. Cut off the top and end of the fruit, then use a knife to score the skin into 4 sections.

2. Place the pomegranate in a bowl of water; break the shell apart along the scored lines.

3. Use your fingers to loosen the arils under water; the seeds will sink, and the white membrane will float. Toss the membrane.

4. Strain through a sieve to catch arils. Eat the seeds as they are, or sprinkle them over salads, grilled meats, or fish dishes.

Sunshine Fruit Salad

Assemble the night before, but stir in and sprinkle with sliced almonds just before serving.

SERVES **6**   ACTIVE **25 MIN.**   TOTAL **25 MIN.**

—

1 cup orange sections (from about 3 oranges)

1 cup grapefruit sections (from about 2 grapefruits)

½ cup pomegranate arils

4 kiwifruit, peeled and sliced

1 (4-lb.) pineapple, peeled and cut into 1-inch cubes

1 tsp. lemon zest, plus 1 Tbsp. fresh lemon juice

1 Tbsp. fresh orange juice

½ cup sliced almonds, toasted and divided

Greek yogurt (optional)

1. Combine first 5 ingredients in a medium bowl. Combine lemon zest and citrus juices in a small bowl. Gently stir lemon mixture into fruit; cover and chill.

2. Just before serving, stir ¼ cup almonds into the fruit mixture. Serve with a dollop of yogurt, if desired, and sprinkle remaining almonds on each serving.

Tasty Swap

Make this a Berry Fruit Salad by swapping 1 cup fresh blueberries and 1 cup fresh raspberries for the citrus sections called for here.

Cherry-Pie Spice Coffee Cake

The convenience of spice blends like the pie spice used in this good-to-the-last-crumb cake means you don't have to keep a half dozen jars that you may only rarely use on hand. Pie spice is made of allspice, cinnamon, cloves, ginger, and nutmeg. Think beyond pies and cakes and use it in rubs for meat or add it to apple juice to make a hot, spiced cider.

SERVES **12**   ACTIVE **25 MIN.**   TOTAL **1 HOUR, 10 MIN., PLUS 1 HOUR, 15 MIN. COOLING**

¾ cup toasted chopped pecans

½ tsp. pumpkin pie spice

3¼ cups (about 14 oz.) all-purpose flour, divided, plus more for pan

1¼ cups packed light brown sugar, divided

1 tsp. kosher salt, divided

⅓ cup unsalted butter, melted

Vegetable shortening, for greasing pan

1 cup frozen pitted cherries

1 cup granulated sugar, divided

¾ cup unsalted butter, softened

2 large eggs

1 large egg yolk

2 tsp. vanilla extract

2 tsp. baking powder

¼ tsp. baking soda

1 (8-oz.) container full-fat Greek yogurt

1. Stir together pecans, pie spice, ¾ cup of the flour, ¾ cup of the brown sugar, and ½ teaspoon of the salt in a bowl. Stir in melted butter. Freeze until hardened, about 20 minutes.

2. Meanwhile, preheat oven to 350°F. Grease a 10-inch tube pan with shortening; dust pan with flour. Pulse cherries and ¼ cup of the granulated sugar in a food processor until finely chopped, 6 to 8 times. Transfer to a bowl; chill until ready to use.

3. Beat softened butter, remaining ½ cup brown sugar, and remaining ¾ cup granulated sugar with a stand mixer fitted with a paddle attachment on medium-high until light and fluffy, 2 minutes. Add eggs and yolk 1 at a time, beating well on low after each addition. Stir in vanilla.

4. Stir together baking powder, baking soda, remaining 2½ cups flour, and remaining ½ teaspoon salt in a bowl. Add flour mixture to softened butter mixture alternately with yogurt in 3 additions (beginning and ending with flour mixture), beating on low just until combined after each addition.

5. Stir ¾ cup of the batter into chilled cherry mixture. Spoon half of the remaining plain batter into prepared pan. Spoon cranberry-batter mixture over, smoothing into an even layer. Top with remaining plain batter. Crumble frozen pecan-pie spice mixture into chunks. Sprinkle evenly over cake.

6. Bake in preheated oven until a wooden pick inserted in center comes out clean, 45 to 55 minutes, tenting with aluminum foil after 35 minutes, if needed, to prevent excessive browning. Cool in pan on a wire rack 15 minutes. Remove from pan. Cool completely on rack, 1 hour.

Pecan Praline Lattes

One of the South's favorite candy confections collides with your morning cup of coffee for a dreamy, luscious candy-kissed latte.

SERVES **6**   ACTIVE **10 MIN.**   TOTAL **10 MIN.**

---

4 cups hot brewed coffee

1 cup firmly packed dark brown sugar

1 cup half-and-half

1 cup praline syrup

Sweetened whipped cream

Heat first 3 ingredients in a large saucepan over medium, stirring constantly, until heated through. (Do not boil.) Stir in syrup. Pour into warm mugs and serve with sweetened whipped cream.

JUMPSTART!

Make the latte mix first thing and keep it hot in an insulated pitcher or thermos.

COZY WINTER SUPPER

Comforting and delicious for when company is coming over or family is headed to town, the beauty of this menu is that it can be made mostly in advance. Plus, the lasagna "bakes" in a slow cooker so you can be a hands-off chef.

MENU

—

Orchard Mule

Shaved Radish Toasts

Smoky Rosemary Grissini

Wedge Salad with Creamy Blue Cheese Dressing

Slow-Cooker Butternut & Sausage Lasagna

Brownie Mousse Stacks

Orchard Mule

This autumnal spin on the Moscow mule has lots of crisp apple flavor. Woodsy rosemary complements the fruit and is a pretty drink stir.

SERVES **1**   ACTIVE **5 MIN.**   TOTAL **5 MIN.**

1 tsp. fresh lemon juice (from 1 lemon)

3 Tbsp. (1½ oz.) vodka

¼ cup (2 oz.) apple cider

⅓ cup (4 oz.) ginger beer

Apple slice

Rosemary sprig

Combine the lemon juice, vodka, cider, and ginger beer in an ice-filled copper mug. Stir. Garnish with an apple slice and a rosemary sprig for stirring.

Make It a Mocktail

Increase the amount of apple cider and ginger beer to replace the vodka.

Shaved Radish Toasts

This quick twist on crostini combines thinly sliced radishes, flaky sea salt, black pepper, and thyme leaves for an easy, lovely last-minute appetizer.

SERVES **8**   ACTIVE **25 MIN.**
TOTAL **40 MIN., INCLUDING CREAM CHEESE**

24 (½-inch-thick) diagonally cut baguette slices

¼ cup unsalted butter, melted

Buttermilk-Herb Cream Cheese (recipe follows)

Thinly sliced rainbow radishes

Sea salt flakes

Black pepper

Fresh dill leaves

1. Preheat oven to 375°F. Arrange baguette slices in a single layer on a baking sheet. Brush tops with melted butter. Bake until slices are just beginning to brown at edges, about 12 minutes. Remove from oven, and cool to room temperature.

2. Spread 1½ teaspoons Buttermilk-Herb Cream Cheese on each crostini.

3. Top with radishes, sea salt flakes, black pepper, and dill leaves.

Buttermilk-Herb Cream Cheese

8 oz. chive and onion cream cheese, softened

6 Tbsp. whole buttermilk

2 tsp. lemon zest (from 1 lemon)

½ tsp. kosher salt

½ tsp. black pepper

Process cream cheese, buttermilk, lemon zest, salt, and black pepper in a food processor until smooth.

Smoky Rosemary Grissini

MAKES **32**   ACTIVE **20 MIN.**   TOTAL **50 MIN.**

½ (17.3-oz.) pkg. frozen puff pastry sheets, thawed

All-purpose flour, for work surface

1 large egg, lightly beaten

3 oz. Manchego cheese, finely shredded (about 1⅓ cups)

1 tsp. minced rosemary

½ tsp. smoked paprika

½ tsp. flaked smoked salt (such as Maldon)

¼ tsp. black pepper

⅛ tsp. garlic powder

1. Preheat oven to 400°F. Line 2 baking sheets with parchment paper. Transfer puff pastry sheet to a lightly floured work surface; roll into a 16- x 10-inch rectangle (about ⅛ inch thick). Brush dough lightly with egg; reserve remaining egg. Sprinkle Manchego, rosemary, smoked paprika, smoked salt, black pepper, and garlic powder over 1 long half of dough rectangle. Fold empty dough half over cheese mixture; press gently. Cut dough crosswise into 32 (5- x ½-inch) strips. Transfer to prepared baking sheets.

2. Working with 1 strip at a time, brush both sides lightly with reserved egg. Twist and gently stretch each strip to about 7 inches long. Bake in preheated oven until golden, 14 to 16 minutes, rotating baking sheets halfway through bake time. Transfer to a wire rack to cool completely, 15 minutes.

Tasty Swap

Grissini are super versatile; substitute shredded Parmesan, Pecorino-Romano, or Asiago for the Manchego cheese. Change up the herbs and use regular paprika and sea salt if you prefer.

Wedge Salad with Creamy Blue Cheese Dressing

Arrange and dress the wedges on a large platter if you want to serve this pretty salad family-style, or plate the salads individually so that all the yummy garnishes are divided among every plate.

SERVES **8**   ACTIVE **15 MIN.**   TOTAL **15 MIN.**

———

1 cup whole buttermilk

2 garlic cloves, grated

6 Tbsp. mayonnaise

6 Tbsp. sour cream

4 Tbsp. chopped fresh chives

4 Tbsp. chopped fresh flat-leaf parsley

1 cup (4 oz.) crumbled blue cheese, divided

2½ tsp. kosher salt

1 tsp. black pepper

½ tsp. paprika

2 iceberg lettuce heads

1 cup sweety drop peppers, drained and rinsed

¼ cup finely diced red onion

¼ cup flat-leaf parsley leaves

1. Whisk first 6 ingredients in a medium bowl. Stir in ¾ cup crumbled blue cheese and the salt, black pepper, and paprika.

2. Quarter each iceberg lettuce head and divide among 8 plates. Spoon dressing evenly over lettuce. Divide the sweety drop peppers, remaining ¼ cup blue cheese, red onion, and parsley leaves.

Slow-Cooker Butternut & Sausage Lasagna

You'll be surprised how well lasagna cooks up in the slow cooker. Use traditional noodles (not the no-boil kind), and place them in the cooker uncooked for best results.

SERVES **8 TO 10**   ACTIVE **47 MIN.**
TOTAL **4 HOURS, 57 MIN.**

9 oz. part-skim ricotta cheese

½ cup grated Parmesan cheese, divided

2 Tbsp. chopped fresh flat-leaf parsley, divided

1 Tbsp. minced fresh rosemary

¼ tsp. freshly ground black pepper

6 garlic cloves, divided

6 cups water

½ cup red wine vinegar

1 large butternut squash, peeled, seeded, cut into ¼-inch-thick slices

Cooking spray

12 oz. hot Italian sausage links, casings removed

2 cups chopped onion

1 Tbsp. olive oil

3 (3.5-oz.) pkg. shiitake mushrooms, stemmed and sliced

1 cup unsalted chicken stock

½ cup chopped fresh basil leaves

1 (25-oz.) jar marinara sauce

12 uncooked lasagna noodles

4 oz. fontina cheese, shredded and divided (about 1 cup)

Parsley leaves (optional)

1. Combine ricotta, 2 tablespoons Parmesan cheese, 1 tablespoon parsley, rosemary, black pepper, and 1 garlic clove, grated, in a bowl; set aside.

2. Bring 6 cups water to a boil in a large skillet; stir in red wine vinegar. Add squash and cook 3 minutes. Drain.

3. Heat skillet over medium-high. Coat pan with cooking spray. Add sausage; cook 7 minutes, stirring to crumble. Stir in onion; cook 8 minutes or until onion is tender.

4. Heat oil in a large saucepan over medium-high. Add mushrooms; cook 10 minutes or until liquid evaporates. Mince 5 garlic cloves; stir into mushrooms. Stir in stock, basil, and marinara. Bring to a boil; remove from heat.

5. To assemble, spoon 1 cup sauce into the bottom of a 6-quart electric slow cooker. Top with 4 noodles, breaking to fit cooker. Layer half of squash, half of sausage mixture, and ¼ cup fontina cheese over noodles; top with 1 cup sauce. Arrange 4 noodles over sauce; top with ricotta mixture. Sprinkle with ¼ cup fontina; top with remaining half of sausage mixture and remaining half of squash mixture. Arrange remaining 4 noodles over squash mixture; top with remaining 1½ cups sauce and ¼ cup fontina. Cover and cook on LOW for 4 hours.

6. Preheat broiler. Uncover slow cooker; sprinkle lasagna with remaining ¼ cup fontina and remaining 2 tablespoons Parmesan. Broil on middle rack of oven 2 minutes or until cheese browns. Sprinkle with remaining parsley and parsley leaves, if desired. Let stand 10 minutes before serving.

Brownie Mousse Stacks

A trio of chocolate—dark, milk, and white—collide in this rich-yet-airy dessert.
Allow plenty of time to make fillings and assemble stacks. You can chill
the assembled stacks up to 24 hours ahead of serving time.

SERVES **8**   ACTIVE **45 MIN.**   TOTAL **4 HOURS, 30 MIN.**

—

BROWNIES

Vegetable cooking spray

¾ cup butter

**1 (4-oz.) bittersweet dark
chocolate baking bar, chopped**

1½ cups granulated sugar

1 tsp. vanilla extract

4 large eggs

**1 cup (about 4¼ oz.) all-purpose
flour**

¼ tsp. baking powder

¼ tsp. table salt

MILK CHOCOLATE MOUSSE

**½ (12-oz.) pkg. milk chocolate
morsels (1 cup)**

**¼ cup cookie spread (such
as Biscoff)**

1 cup heavy cream

WHITE CHOCOLATE MOUSSE

1 cup white chocolate morsels

1¼ cups heavy cream, divided

ADDITIONAL INGREDIENTS

8 large paper clips

Heavy-duty aluminum foil

**Fresh raspberries, rosemary
leaves, and chocolate curls**

1. Prepare Brownies: Preheat oven to 350°F. Line bottom and sides of a 13- x 9-inch pan with aluminum foil, allowing 2 to 3 inches to extend over sides; lightly grease foil with cooking spray. Microwave butter and chopped bittersweet chocolate in a large microwave-safe bowl at HIGH 1½ to 2 minutes or just until melted and smooth, stirring every 30 seconds. Whisk in sugar and vanilla. Add eggs, 1 at a time, whisking just until blended after each addition. Stir together flour, baking powder, and salt in a small bowl. Whisk flour mixture into chocolate mixture until blended. Pour mixture into prepared pan.

2. Bake in preheated oven 18 to 20 minutes or until a wooden pick inserted in center comes out with a few moist crumbs. Cool completely on a wire rack (about 1 hour). Lift brownies from pan, using foil sides as handles. Cut 8 circles, using a 3-inch round cutter. Reserve scraps for another use.

3. Prepare Milk Chocolate Mousse: Microwave milk chocolate morsels and cookie spread in a small microwave-safe glass bowl at MEDIUM (50% power) 1½ to 2 minutes or until melted and smooth, stirring every 30 seconds. Cool 5 minutes.

4. Beat 1 cup heavy cream at medium speed with an electric mixer until soft peaks form; fold cream into milk chocolate mixture. Chill while making White Chocolate Mousse.

5. Prepare White Chocolate Mousse: Microwave white chocolate morsels and ¼ cup cream in a small microwave-safe glass bowl at MEDIUM (50% power) 1½ to 2 minutes or until melted and smooth, stirring every 30 seconds. Cool 5 minutes.

6. Beat remaining 1 cup cream at medium with an electric mixer until soft peaks form; fold into white chocolate mixture. Chill while preparing foil molds for Step 7.

7. Assemble stacks: Wash and dry paper clips. Cut heavy-duty aluminum foil into 8 (6- x 10-inch) pieces. Fold each piece in half to form a 3- x 10-inch strip. Wrap each strip around a 3-inch-diameter can. (This helps create a smooth curve.) Wrap 1 curved foil strip around each brownie; secure with a large paper clip. Immediately spoon Milk Chocolate Mousse into a zip-top plastic freezer bag. (Do not seal.) Snip 1 corner of bag to make a small hole (about ½ inch). Pipe mousse onto brownies, dividing mixture evenly. Use a small spoon to level gently. Repeat procedure with White Chocolate Mousse. Chill 2 hours; remove foil to serve. Garnish with fresh raspberries, rosemary leaves, and chocolate curls.

JUMPSTART!

Make the brownies up to 2 days ahead; store in an airtight container.

CLASSIC CHRISTMAS FEAST

Whether your family's tradition is to feast on Christmas Eve or gather at the table after the presents have been opened on Christmas Day, this elegant meal is meant to be cooked and lingered over together from the first sip of mulled wine to the last bite of cheesecake.

MENU
—

Mulled White Wine

Pomegranate-Bourbon Smash

Spiced Pecans

Camembert-Chutney Bites

Pear-Green Bean Salad with Sorghum Vinaigrette

Standing Rib Roast with Roasted Vegetables

Buttermilk Fantail Rolls

Lemony Sauteed Broccolini with Garlic

Pumpkin-Chocolate Marble Cheesecake

Mulled White Wine

Red wine is the classic choice, but dry white wine is also delicious served warm with mulling spices. Serve what you most enjoy sipping.

SERVES **8**   ACTIVE **10 MIN.**
TOTAL **1 HOUR, 20 MIN., INCLUDING SYRUP**

——

- **2 (750-ml) bottles dry white wine**
- **8 orange slices**
- **Mulling Syrup (recipe follows)**

Heat the wine in a large saucepan over low until hot, being careful not to boil. Drop an orange slice into the bottom of 8 heatproof glass mugs and add 2 tablespoons Mulling Syrup to each glass. Ladle the warm wine into each mug and serve hot. The syrup is a great gift for the host or favor for guests. Use it to give holiday beverages like wine or apple cider a rich, warm-spiced flavor.

Make It a Mocktail

Substitute white grape juice for the dry white wine.

Mulling Syrup

- **1 orange, thinly sliced, seeds removed**
- **1¼ cups granulated sugar**
- **6 whole cloves**
- **3 cinnamon sticks**
- **¾ tsp. ground nutmeg**

1. Preheat oven to 275°F. Line a baking sheet with parchment. Arrange orange slices in a single layer on baking sheet. Bake until dry, turning once or twice, 50 to 60 minutes. Let cool on wire racks.

2. Combine sugar, cloves, cinnamon, and nutmeg in a large, heavy saucepan. Pour in 4 cups water and stir gently over low heat until sugar has dissolved. Increase heat to medium-high and cook for 20 minutes. Remove from heat and let cool. Strain through a fine-mesh sieve, reserving cinnamon sticks but discarding remaining solids.

3. Have ready 2 sterilized 8.5-oz. bottles. Divide reserved cinnamon sticks and dried oranges between the two bottles. Using a funnel, pour warm syrup into bottles and seal. MAKES ABOUT 2 CUPS

Pomegranate-Bourbon Smash

The spirit of the South gets gussied up with festive fruit and a spicy ginger syrup.

SERVES **12**   ACTIVE **15 MIN.**   TOTAL **1 HOUR, 15 MIN.**

——

HONEY-GINGER SYRUP
- **¾ cup honey**
- **½ cup water**
- **2 Tbsp. chopped fresh ginger (from 1 [1-inch] piece)**
- **1½ tsp. finely minced orange zest (from ½ orange)**

COCKTAIL
- **3 cups pomegranate juice**
- **3 cups (24 oz.) bourbon**
- **⅓ cup fresh orange juice (from 1 large orange)**
- **3 cups ice**
- **2¼ cups seltzer water**
- **12 orange slices**
- **½ cup pomegranate arils**

1. Prepare the Honey-Ginger Syrup: Stir together all the syrup ingredients in a small saucepan. Bring to a boil over medium-high, stirring occasionally. Reduce the heat to medium-low, and simmer, stirring occasionally, until the honey is melted, about 2 minutes. Remove from heat, and let cool to room temperature, about 1 hour. Pour the mixture through a fine mesh strainer, discarding solids. Refrigerate the syrup in an airtight container until ready to use. Store in the refrigerator up to 2 weeks.

2. Prepare the Cocktail: Stir together the pomegranate juice, bourbon, Honey-Ginger Syrup, and orange juice in a large pitcher. Add the ice, and stir well. Gently stir in the seltzer. Serve over ice in old-fashioned glasses. Garnish with an orange slice skewered with a toothpick to form a canoe. Sprinkle the cavity with pomegranate arils and rest the skewer across the rim of the glass.

Tasty Swap

Substitute cranberry juice for the pomegranate juice, if desired. Rye whiskey is a worthy stand-in for bourbon here, too.

Spiced Pecans

Enjoy this classic recipe for snacking or sharing.

SERVES **8** ACTIVE **5 MIN.** TOTAL **10 MIN.**

2 cups shelled pecan halves

1 tsp. cinnamon

2 tsp. chili powder

1 tsp. cumin

½ tsp. cayenne pepper

½ tsp. ground ginger

1 tsp. table salt

3 Tbsp. unsalted butter, melted

2 Tbsp. packed light brown sugar

1. Preheat oven to 400°F. Spread pecans on baking sheet in a single layer. Roast, shaking pan occasionally, until fragrant and light golden brown, about 10 minutes.

2. Combine cinnamon, chili powder, cumin, cayenne, ginger and salt in a small bowl.

3. Remove pecans from oven and place in a bowl. Toss with melted butter, brown sugar and spice mix while still hot, combining evenly. Let cool and serve.

Camembert–Chutney Bites

This simple, savory-meets-sweet appetizer packs a lot of flavor and texture into a single bite.

SERVES **12 (SERVING SIZE: 2 BITES)**
ACTIVE **10 MIN.** TOTAL **18 MIN.**

24 frozen mini phyllo pastry shells, thawed

3 oz. Camembert cheese, rind removed

2 Tbsp. tomato chutney (such as Alecia's Tomato Chutney)

24 toasted pecan halves

1 tsp. smoked flaky sea salt

1. Preheat oven to 350°F. Arrange pastry shells on a rimmed baking sheet.

2. Cut Camembert into 24 very small pieces. Spoon ¼ teaspoon chutney into each shell; top evenly with cheese pieces and pecans.

3. Bake in preheated oven until cheese is melted, 7 to 8 minutes. Sprinkle with salt; serve immediately.

Pear-Green Bean Salad with Sorghum Vinaigrette

This recipe shows why mixing your fruit with your vegetables is a good thing!

SERVES **8** ACTIVE **15 MIN.**
TOTAL **20 MIN., INCLUDING VINAIGRETTE**

8 oz. haricots verts (thin green beans), trimmed

1 (5-oz.) pkg. gourmet mixed salad greens

2 red Bartlett pears, cut into thin strips

½ small red onion, sliced

4 oz. Gorgonzola cheese, crumbled

1 cup toasted pecans or Spiced Pecans (recipe at left)

Sorghum Vinaigrette (recipe follows)

Cook beans in boiling salted water to cover 3 to 4 minutes or until crisp-tender; drain. Plunge beans into ice water to stop the cooking process; drain. Toss together salad greens, next 4 ingredients, and beans. Serve with Sorghum Vinaigrette.

Sorghum Vinaigrette

½ cup sorghum syrup

½ cup malt or apple cider vinegar

3 Tbsp. bourbon

2 tsp. grated onion

1 tsp. table salt

1 tsp. freshly ground black pepper

½ tsp. hot sauce

1 cup olive oil

Whisk together first 7 ingredients until blended. Add oil in a slow, steady stream, whisking until smooth.

Tasty Swap

No sorghum syrup? No problem. Corn syrup, honey, maple syrup or molasses are all sweet substitutions for the sorghum syrup in this vinaigrette.

Standing Rib Roast with Roasted Vegetables

Prepare for "oohs" and "ahhs" when you place this roast on your holiday table. Although it looks difficult, it's truly simple to prepare—slather it with the herb butter the night before; then let your oven do the work. A bit of tangy verjus—the pressed juice of unripened grapes—is the secret ingredient in the rich, flavorful gravy. Substitute wine vinegar if you wish.

SERVES **10** ACTIVE **40 MIN.**
TOTAL **17 HOURS, INCLUDING 12 HOURS CHILLING, VEGETABLES, AND GRAVY**

▬

- ½ cup salted butter, softened
- 1 Tbsp. coarsely ground dried green peppercorns
- 1 Tbsp. coarsely ground pink peppercorns
- 2 Tbsp. kosher salt
- 1½ Tbsp. chopped fresh rosemary, plus more for garnish
- 1½ Tbsp. chopped fresh marjoram or oregano
- 1 Tbsp. extra-virgin olive oil
- 1 (8-lb.) 4-rib prime rib roast, chine bone removed
- Roasted Vegetables (recipe follows)
- Verjus Pan-Gravy (recipe follows)

1. Stir together butter, peppercorns, salt, rosemary, marjoram or oregano, and oil in a small bowl. Spread evenly over roast. Chill, uncovered, 12 hours or up to 24 hours.

2. Remove roast from the refrigerator; let stand at room temperature 1 hour.

3. Preheat oven to 450°F. Place roast on a lightly greased rack in a roasting pan. Bake on lowest oven rack 45 minutes. Reduce oven temperature to 350°F; bake until a meat thermometer inserted in thickest portion registers 120°F to 130°F for medium-rare or 130°F to 135°F for medium, about 1 hour and 30 minutes.

4. Let stand 30 minutes. Transfer roast to a serving platter, reserving ½ cup drippings for gravy. Serve with roasted vegetables and pan-gravy. Garnish with rosemary.

Roasted Vegetables

- 1 lb. small rainbow carrots with tops, trimmed and peeled
- 1 lb. parsnips, peeled and cut lengthwise into 3-inch pieces
- 8 oz. French breakfast radishes, trimmed and halved lengthwise
- 8 oz. Chioggia beets (candy cane beets), peeled and cut into 1-inch wedges
- 2 Tbsp. chopped fresh rosemary
- 2 Tbsp. olive oil
- 2 tsp. kosher salt
- 1 tsp. black pepper

Preheat oven to 400°F. Toss together all ingredients in a large bowl. Spread in a single layer in a 17- x 11-inch rimmed baking pan. Bake until tender, about 45 minutes, stirring every 15 minutes. Serve with roast.

Verjus Pan-Gravy

- ½ cup drippings from Standing Rib Roast with Roasted Vegetables
- ½ cup chopped yellow onion (from 1 onion)
- ½ cup (about 2⅛ oz.) all-purpose flour
- 4 to 5 cups beef broth
- 1½ Tbsp. verjus
- ¼ tsp. kosher salt
- ¼ tsp. black pepper

1. Heat pan drippings in a medium saucepan over medium. Add onions, and cook, stirring occasionally, until tender, about 5 minutes. Sprinkle flour over onions, stirring constantly; cook, stirring constantly, until flour is golden brown, about 2 minutes.

2. Gradually whisk in 4 cups of the broth. Cook, stirring often, just until mixture comes to a boil and is smooth and thick, about 5 minutes. If mixture is too thick, add up to 1 cup broth, ¼ cup at a time, until mixture reaches desired consistency. Stir in verjus, salt, and pepper. Serve with roast and vegetables.

TEST KITCHEN TIP: To ensure smooth gravy, stir the flour until dissolved in a small amount of the cold broth before adding it to the gravy. Then add the rest of the broth, cook, and stir constantly with a wire whisk until the gravy thickens.

Buttermilk Fantail Rolls

It wouldn't be a holiday feast without a fresh batch of homemade bread. These buttery rolls with golden, pull-apart layers are finished off with sprinkles of flaky salt. The best part is that they can be baked in advance.

MAKES **2 DOZEN**   ACTIVE **45 MIN.**
TOTAL **10 HOURS, 15 MIN.**

½ cup warm water (105°F to 110°F)

2 (¼-oz.) envelopes active dry yeast

6 Tbsp. plus 1 tsp. granulated sugar, divided

2 large eggs, lightly beaten

1 cup whole buttermilk, at room temperature

1¼ tsp. kosher salt

½ cup plus 2 Tbsp. unsalted butter, melted and divided

3¾ to 4 cups (about 17 oz.) all-purpose flour, divided

¼ cup unsalted butter, softened and divided

Flaky sea salt (such as Maldon)

1. Combine warm water, yeast, and 1 teaspoon of the sugar in a 1-cup liquid measuring cup; let stand until foamy, about 5 minutes.

2. Stir together eggs, buttermilk, kosher salt, ½ cup of the melted butter, and remaining 6 tablespoons sugar in a medium bowl. Add yeast mixture and 3½ cups of the flour; stir until a dough forms. Sprinkle a work surface with ¼ cup of the flour; turn dough out onto floured surface, and knead until smooth and slightly elastic, about 4 minutes, adding up to an additional ¼ cup flour, if needed. Place dough in a lightly greased bowl; turn to grease top. Cover with plastic wrap, and chill 8 to 24 hours.

3. Coat 2 (12-cup) muffin pans with cooking spray. Punch chilled dough down, and turn out onto a lightly floured surface. Divide dough in half. Roll 1 dough half into a 16- x 12-inch rectangle (about ¼ inch thick). Brush top with 2 tablespoons of the softened butter. Starting from a 12-inch side, cut dough into 6 (2-inch-wide) strips. Cut dough strips crosswise into quarters. (You will have 24 [4- x 2-inch] dough pieces.)

4. Stack 3 dough pieces together, buttered side up. Top with a fourth piece, buttered side down. Repeat with remaining 20 dough pieces, making 6 stacks. Cut each stack in half crosswise, making a total of 12 stacks of 2-inch squares. Place 1 stack on its side, layers facing up, in each muffin cup. Cover loosely with plastic wrap. Repeat process with remaining dough half, 2 tablespoons softened butter, and muffin pan. Let rolls rise in a warm (80°F to 85°F) place, free from drafts, until doubled in size, about 1 hour.

5. Preheat oven to 375°F. Bake rolls until golden brown, 12 to 15 minutes. Brush rolls with remaining 2 tablespoons melted butter, and sprinkle with desired amount of sea salt.

JUMPSTART!

The dough for Buttermilk Fantail Rolls is very easy to work with, but it needs to rise twice, so be sure to allow enough time. Or bake the rolls a day ahead, reserving the melted butter and sea salt in Step 5. Let them cool, and store in a zip-top plastic bag. Reheat in a 300°F oven 10 minutes, or until warm. Brush warm rolls with melted butter, and top with sea salt.

Lemony Sauteed Broccolini with Garlic

This dish is a fast, fresh take on the usual long-simmered green beans or steamed asparagus, substituting slender stalks of broccolini instead.

SERVES **8**   ACTIVE **10 MIN.**   TOTAL **20 MIN.**

---

2 Tbsp. olive oil

4 garlic cloves, thinly sliced

2 lb. broccolini, washed and trimmed

⅓ cup white wine

1 Tbsp grated lemon rind

2 Tbsp. fresh lemon juice (from 1 lemon)

¼ to ½ tsp. crushed red pepper

¾ tsp. kosher salt

¾ tsp. black pepper

Heat oil in a Dutch oven over medium. Add garlic; cook, stirring often, until garlic is golden brown and crispy, about 1 minute. Add broccolini; cook 4 minutes, stirring occasionally. Stir in wine. Cover, reduce heat to medium-low, and cook 6 minutes or until tender-crisp. Stir in lemon rind, lemon juice, ¼ teaspoon crushed red pepper, salt and black pepper. Toss. Stir in an additional ¼ teaspoon crushed red pepper, if desired.

Pumpkin-Chocolate Marble Cheesecake

Dense and luscious, pumpkin makes cheesecake extra moist, rich, and oh-so-flavorful.

SERVES **12**   ACTIVE **10 MIN.**   TOTAL **3 HOURS, 45 MIN., INCLUDING CHILLING**

——

ENTERTAIN

15 whole graham crackers, broken into small pieces

⅓ cup granulated sugar

6 Tbsp. unsalted butter, melted

4 oz. bittersweet chocolate, chopped

1 (16-oz.) container cottage cheese (2 cups)

2 (8-oz.) pkg. cream cheese, at room temperature

2 cups packed light brown sugar

3 large eggs

¼ cup all-purpose flour

1 (15-oz.) can pure pumpkin

2 tsp. ground ginger

1 tsp. cinnamon

½ tsp. nutmeg

2 tsp. vanilla extract

¼ tsp. table salt

1. Preheat oven to 375°F; butter a 10-inch nonstick springform pan.

2. Blend graham crackers and sugar in a food processor until ground. Pulse in butter to blend. Press mixture over bottom and 1 inch up side of pan. Bake until lightly browned, about 15 minutes. Let cool on a wire rack. Reduce oven temperature to 325°F. Wrap bottom and side of springform with 2 layers of foil.

3. Melt chocolate in a bowl set over a pan of simmering water.

4. Blend cottage cheese in a food processor until smooth. Add cream cheese, sugar, eggs and flour; process until smooth. Transfer to a bowl; stir in pumpkin, ginger, cinnamon, nutmeg, vanilla and salt.

5. Stir about 1½ cups of batter into melted chocolate. Pour remaining batter into springform. Drop large spoonfuls of chocolate mixture over batter; use tip of a sharp knife to make decorative swirls.

6. Bring a kettle of water to a boil. Place springform in a large roasting pan. Transfer to oven. Carefully pour in boiling water to reach halfway up side of springform. Bake at 325°F until cake is just firm in the center and cheesecake starts to pull away from side of springform, about 1½ hours. Remove springform from roasting pan; let cool completely on a wire rack. Cover and chill for at least 2 hours before serving. (Can be made up to 3 days ahead. Cover and chill.)

Tasty Swap

If you don't like the idea of chocolate in your pumpkin pie, change this recipe up by substituting 4 oz. butterscotch morsels, caramel morsels, or white chocolate chips for the chopped chocolate called for here.

'TWAS THE NIGHT AFTER CHRISTMAS SUPPER

When you've got leftovers, you've got delicious opportunities! This menu was created using leftovers from the Classic Christmas Feast menu (page 99), but it's equally delicious prepared from scratch—no leftovers required.

MENU
—

Hot Pomegranate-Apple Cider

Cheesy Bread with Herbs

Next-Day Beef Stroganoff

Mulled Wine-Poached Pears

Hot Pomegranate-Apple Cider

This is a tasty way to use leftover pomegranate juice from making Pomegranate-Bourbon Smash cocktails (page 100), but you can also substitute cranberry, cran-apple, even tart cherry juice here. For an alcoholic cider, add 1½ ounces of bourbon or spiced rum to each 8 ounces of hot cider.

MAKES **8 CUPS**   ACTIVE **10 MIN.**
TOTAL **1 HOUR, 10 MIN.**

---

2 cups pomegranate juice

6 cups apple cider

4 allspice berries

4 whole cloves

2 star anise pods, plus more for garnish

2 cinnamon sticks, plus more for serving

Dehydrated apple slices, plus more for serving

Bring everything to a boil in a medium saucepan over high heat. Boil 1 minute then remove and let steep 1 hour. Strain and discard solids. Return to the saucepan and keep warm over low heat. Ladle into mugs and serve with additional dehydrated apple slices and a cinnamon stick.

Cheesy Bread with Herbs

Use leftover Buttermilk Fantail Rolls (page 107) or any leftover dinner rolls to make this ooey, gooey, cheesy pull-apart bread.

SERVES **6**   ACTIVE **10 MIN.**   TOTAL **20 MIN.**

---

8 leftover Buttermilk Fantail Rolls (page 107) or other day-old rolls

⅓ cup salted butter, melted

3 garlic cloves, minced

1 Tbsp. chopped fresh flat-leaf parsley

½ tsp. crushed red pepper

1½ oz. mozzarella cheese, shredded (about ⅓ cup)

1 oz. Parmesan cheese, grated (about ¼ cup)

1. Preheat the oven to 350°F. Lightly coat an 8- x 4-inch loaf pan with cooking spray.

2. Cut an "x" in the top of each roll and arrange them cut-side up in the loaf pan.

3. Mix together the butter, garlic, parsley, and red pepper flakes and drizzle the mixture over the slits in the rolls. Sprinkle the mozzarella and Parmesan evenly over the surface. Cover with foil. Bake in preheated oven 15 minutes. Remove the foil and bake 5 minutes more or until cheese is melted and tops of rolls are lightly brown. Serve immediately.

Next-Day Beef Stroganoff

This satisfying, cold winter night dish is super easy to make with leftover beef and roasted veggies from the Standing Rib Roast with Roasted Vegetables (page 103). You can also start from scratch by cooking 1½ pounds of cubed beef sirloin, or turning to the convenience of packaged cooked beef strips from the grocery store refrigerator case. No leftover veggies? No worries. Simply up the amount of onions to 2 and sliced mushrooms to equal 1½ cups instead.

SERVES **4**   ACTIVE **10 MIN.**   TOTAL **30 MIN.**

1 (12-oz.) pkg. wide egg noodles

1 Tbsp. olive oil

1 small red onion, thinly sliced

½ tsp. kosher salt

½ cup sliced button mushrooms

2 cups cubed leftover Roasted Vegetables (page 103)

4 cups cubed leftover beef from Standing Rib Roast with Roasted Vegetables (page 103)

1 8-oz. container sour cream

2½ Tbsp. steak sauce

Chopped fresh flat-leaf parsley

1. Cook the noodles according to the package directions.

2. In a large saucepan heat the oil over medium. Add the onion and salt and cook for 5 minutes. Add the mushrooms and leftover cubed vegetables and cook for 5 minutes. Add the leftover cubed beef and cook until warmed through, about 8 minutes.

3. In a small bowl, combine the sour cream and steak sauce and stir the mixture into the beef and vegetables. Divide the drained noodles among individual plates and top with the stroganoff. Sprinkle each with parsley and serve immediately.

Tasty Swap

Sure, egg noodles are a classic base for this creamy beef stroganoff, but it is equally delicious served over steamed rice, mashed russet or sweet potatoes, spiralized butternut squash "noodles," or wilted angel hair cabbage slaw for five more ways to enjoy your leftovers.

ENTERTAIN

Mulled Wine-Poached Pears

Add this short recipe to the back of the gift tag when giving bottles
of the homemade Mulling Syrup (page 100).

SERVES **4**   ACTIVE **25 MIN.**   TOTAL **1 HOUR, 25 MIN., INCLUDING COOLING**

4 ripe pears, halved lengthwise

1 cup Mulling Syrup (page 100)

½ bottle dry white wine

Vanilla ice cream

¼ cup sliced almonds

1. Arrange pears in medium saucepan. Whisk together syrup, wine and ¼ cup water. Pour over pears. Bring to a simmer and cook over low heat until pears are easily pierced with a knife, 10 to 15 minutes.

2. Transfer the pears with a slotted spoon to a platter and tent loosely with foil. Boil the liquid until it is reduced to about ¾ cup. Cool completely and then refrigerate at least 1 hour.

3. Place a scoop of vanilla ice cream in each of 4 bowls. Arrange 2 pear halves on top. Spoon chilled syrup over each. Sprinkle with sliced almonds to serve.

Tasty Swap

Pears are a classic fruit for poaching, but this method works well with other fruit you may have gotten in gift baskets this holiday. Substitute apples, Asian pears, quince, or firm Fuyu persimmons for the pears.

Savor &

Share

A HOLIDAY COOKBOOK

BEST DRESSED

Salads aren't just for hot summer days. Celebrate the bounty of crisp winter greens, fruits, and vegetables with hearty salads served on the side, or as the mouthwatering main attraction.

Fuyu Persimmon, Celery, & Kale with Bacon & Goat Cheese Crumbles

Fuyu persimmons are a round, crisp variety of persimmons that are less astringent than the oval-shaped Hachiya variety. This tasty cool-season fruit is a nice change of pace from the more typical pear or apple in salads.

SERVES **8**   ACTIVE **15 MIN.**   TOTAL **15 MIN.**

- 2 bunches Lacinato kale, stems removed and roughly chopped (6 cups)
- 8 celery stalks, whites to leafy greens, thinly sliced (about 3½ cups)
- 1 Fuyu persimmon, thinly sliced
- 4 cooked bacon slices, crumbled (reserve 1½ Tbsp. bacon drippings)
- 2 oz. goat cheese, crumbled (about ½ cup)

- 3 Tbsp. fresh lemon juice (from 1 lemon)
- 2 Tbsp. finely chopped shallot
- 1 tsp. grainy Dijon mustard
- ¾ tsp. freshly cracked black pepper, divided
- ½ tsp. flaky sea salt, divided
- 3 Tbsp. extra-virgin olive oil

1. Combine kale, celery, and persimmon in a large bowl. Reserve 3 tablespoons each of bacon and goat cheese. Add remaining bacon and goat cheese to kale mixture.

2. Combine fresh lemon juice, shallot, mustard, reserved bacon drippings, ½ teaspoon of the black pepper, and ¼ teaspoon of the salt in a small jar with a lid. Place lid on jar, and shake well to combine, about 30 seconds.

3. Add olive oil to jar. Place lid on jar, and shake until emulsified. Pour dressing over salad, and toss to combine. Sprinkle salad with reserved bacon and goat cheese and remaining ¼ teaspoon each black pepper and salt. Serve immediately.

Dress It Up with Cheese!

Whether you pick mild, fresh cheese, more strongly flavored ripened cheese, or hard, aged cheese to add to your salad, just do it. Cheese adds complexity, texture, and richness that elevates leafy greens to satisfying heights. A few delicious options to try:

YOUNG FRESH CHEESES like goat cheese, burrata, fromage blanc, mozzarella di bufala, mascarpone, and ricotta

SOFT-RIPENED CHEESES, such as Brie, Brillat Savarin, Camembert, Fromager D'Affinois, Humboldt Fog, Pierre Robert, and Robiola

DRIER AGED CHEESES, including cheddar, Grana Padano, Gouda, Gruyère, Manchego, Parmesan, Pecorino, and Asiago

Dress It Up with Fruit!

Of course dried fruit can be added to salads year-round, but there are so many fresh cool-season fruits to incorporate as juicy additions to salads this time of year. Here is a bushel of our favorites:

- APPLES
- AVOCADOS
- CITRUS
- KIWIFRUIT
- PEARS
- PERSIMMONS
- POMEGRANATES

Beet, Fennel, & Asian Pear Salad

Choose red or golden beets, or look for red-and-white-striped Chioggia beets (also called candy cane beets) for a colorful presentation. If you grow tender-leaved chervil, or can find it in your supermarket, substitute it for the parsley here.

SERVES **6** ACTIVE **10 MIN.** TOTAL **55 MIN.**

—

- 2 medium-size beets (about 4 to 6 oz. each)
- 1 small fennel bulb, trimmed (about 5 oz.), halved lengthwise and cored (fronds reserved)
- 1 medium-size Asian pear (about 8 oz.), halved and cored
- 4 cups firmly packed arugula (about 5 oz.)
- ¼ cup firmly packed fresh flat-leaf parsley or chervil leaves
- ¼ cup firmly packed fresh mint leaves
- ¼ cup extra-virgin olive oil
- 2 Tbsp. Champagne vinegar
- 1 tsp. orange zest plus 1 Tbsp. fresh juice (from 1 orange)
- ¾ tsp. kosher salt
- ½ tsp. honey
- ¼ tsp. black pepper

1. Place beets in a medium saucepan with cold water to cover. Bring to a boil over high; reduce heat to low, and simmer until beets are tender, 35 to 40 minutes. Drain and let stand until cool enough to handle, about 15 minutes. Peel beets, and cut into wedges.

2. While beets are cooling, use a mandoline or sharp knife to cut fennel bulb and Asian pear into very thin slices. Place in a large bowl with beet wedges, arugula, parsley or chervil, mint, and reserved fennel fronds.

3. Whisk together oil, vinegar, zest, juice, salt, honey, and pepper in a small bowl. Drizzle vinaigrette over beet mixture, and toss to coat. Serve immediately.

JUMPSTART!

Tossing together a salad is easy if you always have homemade vinaigrette on hand. Find one you love, and double or triple the recipe. Store it in a canning jar in your refrigerator up to 1 week. Just shake, pour, and toss!

Shredded Rainbow Chard Salad with Pancetta & Dates

The vivid yellow, orange, and pink stalks of rainbow chards really brighten up the salad bowl, and the earthy flavor of the leaves provides a nice backdrop for sweet dates and salty pancetta.

SERVES **8**   ACTIVE **15 MIN.**   TOTAL **45 MIN.**

---

3 Tbsp. olive oil

2 Tbsp. red wine vinegar

1 tsp. Dijon mustard

1 tsp. lemon juice

¼ tsp. table salt

¼ tsp. freshly ground black pepper

1 small shallot, minced

3 cups shredded rainbow Swiss chard

11 pitted Medjool dates, thinly sliced

3 oz. cubed cooked pancetta

Whisk together olive oil, vinegar, mustard, lemon juice, salt, pepper, and shallot in a large serving bowl until emulsified. Add the chard and toss to coat. Cover and chill 30 minutes. Toss in the sliced dates and pancetta just before serving.

TEST KITCHEN TIP: Pancetta (pan CHEH tuh) is Italian bacon cured with salt, pepper, and other spices rather than with smoke. Pancetta comes in a roll and can be sliced or chopped. It adds subtle flavor to soups, sauces, meats, and vegetables. Substitute bacon if you prefer a touch of smokiness here.

Dress It Up with Crunch!

Adding a crispy counterpoint to tender leafy green salads is a simple way to add pleasing texture to the mix. Here are a few of our favorite add-ins and toss-ons to dress up any salad:

TOASTED NUTS AND SEEDS

CROUTONS

FLASH-FRIED HERB LEAVES

FRIED ONIONS

SHOESTRING POTATOES

TORTILLA CHIP STRIPS

CHEESE CRISPS OR FRICO

BACON CRUMBLES

UNCOOKED RAMEN NOODLES

SIDES SHOW

Ask someone to name a favorite Thanksgiving or Christmas dish and it's quite likely it will be a side dish rather than the star of the show. If you're looking for the "three" to pair with your "meat-and-" or just an accompaniment for Sunday's roast chicken, we've got you covered.

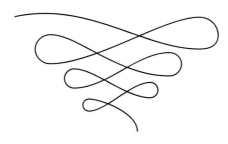

Twice-Baked Potatoes

These fluffy, cheesy, stuffed potatoes are so good, we say bake twice, but eat often!

SERVES **16**   ACTIVE **30 MIN.**   TOTAL **1 HOUR, 45 MIN.**

—

8 medium-size baking potatoes (about 4 lb.)

Canola oil

½ cup butter, cut into slices

1 (8-oz.) container sour cream

8 thick-cut apple-smoked bacon slices, cooked and crumbled

½ cup milk

½ tsp. seasoned salt

½ tsp. black pepper

4 oz. white Cheddar cheese, grated (about 1 cup)

¼ cup sliced chives

4 oz. blue cheese, crumbled (about 1 cup)

1. Preheat oven to 400°F. Rub potatoes with oil. Bake on a baking sheet 45 to 50 minutes or until potatoes are tender and skins are crisp.

2. Meanwhile, stir together butter and next 5 ingredients in a large bowl.

3. Remove potatoes from oven, and let cool 15 minutes. Reduce oven temperature to 300°F. Cut warm potatoes in half lengthwise, and carefully scoop out pulp into bowl with butter mixture, leaving potato shells intact.

4. Mash pulp and butter mixture together using a potato masher. Stir in cheddar cheese, chives, and additional seasoned salt and black pepper to taste. Spoon mixture into potato shells; place on baking sheet. Sprinkle with blue cheese.

5. Bake at 300°F for 15 to 20 minutes or until cheese is melted and potatoes are thoroughly heated.

Tasty Swap

If you love twice-baked baking potatoes, make this recipe with sweet potatoes instead for a colorful change of pace.

Creamed Greens

Kale stands in for the usual spinach or collards in this comforting, creamy side dish.

SERVES **8 TO 10**   ACTIVE **1 HOUR, 10 MIN.**
TOTAL **1 HOUR, 32 MIN., INCLUDING SAUCE**

4½ lb. fresh Lacinato kale*

1 pound bacon slices, chopped

¼ cup butter

2 large onions, diced

3 cups chicken broth

½ cup apple cider vinegar

1 tsp. table salt

½ tsp. black pepper

Béchamel Sauce (recipe follows)

1. Rinse greens. Trim and discard thick stems from bottom of kale leaves (about 2 inches); coarsely chop collard greens.

2. Cook bacon, in batches, in an 8-qt. stockpot over medium heat 10 to 12 minutes or until crisp. Remove bacon, and drain on paper towels, reserving drippings in stockpot. Reserve ¼ cup cooked bacon.

3. Add butter and onions to hot drippings in stockpot. Cook onions, stirring often, 8 minutes or until tender. Add kale, in batches, and cook, stirring occasionally, 5 minutes or until wilted. Stir in chicken broth and next 3 ingredients. Add remaining bacon.

4. Bring to a boil. Reduce heat to low, and cook, stirring occasionally, 15 minutes or to desired degree of tenderness. Drain collards, reserving 1 cup liquid.

5. Stir in Béchamel Sauce. Stir in reserved cooking liquid, ¼ cup at a time, to desired consistency. Transfer to a serving dish, and sprinkle with reserved ¼ cup bacon.

NOTE: *2 (1-lb.) packages fresh kale, trimmed and chopped, may be substituted.

Béchamel Sauce

½ cup butter

2 medium shallots, minced

2 garlic cloves, pressed

¾ cup (about 3¼ oz.) all-purpose flour

4 cups whole milk

½ tsp. table salt

½ tsp. black pepper

¼ tsp. ground nutmeg

1. Melt butter in a heavy saucepan over low heat; add shallots and garlic, and cook 1 minute. Whisk in flour until smooth. Cook, whisking constantly, 1 minute.

2. Increase heat to medium. Gradually whisk in milk; cook, whisking constantly, 5 to 7 minutes or until sauce mixture is thickened and bubbly. Stir in salt, pepper, and nutmeg. MAKES ABOUT 4½ CUPS

JUMPSTART!

Sauce can be made ahead and stored in an airtight container in the refrigerator up to 2 days; warm over low heat before using.

Pecan-Herb Cornbread Dressing

Great Southern-style dressing starts with skillet-cooked cornbread to get that crisp, golden crust. Prepare the cornbread up to two days in advance so that it can dry out completely.

SERVES **15**   ACTIVE **40 MIN.**   TOTAL **3 HOURS**

CORNBREAD

2 cups self-rising white cornmeal mix

1 tsp. granulated sugar (optional)

2 large eggs

2 cups buttermilk

3 Tbsp. salted butter

DRESSING

½ cup salted butter

3 cups chopped sweet onion (from 2 large onions)

2 cups chopped celery (from 6 stalks)

2 Tbsp. chopped fresh sage

2 tsp. chopped fresh thyme

2 tsp. chopped fresh rosemary

6 large eggs

1 (14-oz.) pkg. herb-seasoned stuffing mix (such as Pepperidge Farm)

1½ cups chopped toasted pecans

½ cup chopped fresh flat-leaf parsley

10 cups chicken broth

2 tsp. black pepper

1 tsp. kosher salt

Fresh herb leaves (such as sage, thyme, and rosemary)

1. Prepare the Cornbread: Preheat oven to 425°F. Combine self-rising cornmeal mix and, if desired, sugar in a large bowl. Stir together eggs and buttermilk in a medium bowl; add to cornmeal mixture, stirring just until moistened.

2. Place butter in a 10-inch cast-iron skillet; place skillet in the oven for 5 minutes. Stir melted butter into batter. Pour batter into hot skillet.

3. Bake in preheated oven until cornbread is golden, about 25 minutes; cool in skillet 20 minutes. Remove from skillet to a wire rack, and cool completely, 20 to 30 more minutes. Crumble cornbread. Reduce oven heat to 350°F. (If desired, freeze in a large heavy-duty zip-top plastic bag up to 1 month. Thaw in refrigerator.)

4. Prepare the Dressing: Melt butter in a large skillet over medium-high; add onion and celery, and cook, stirring often, until tender, 10 to 12 minutes. Add sage, thyme, and rosemary and cook, stirring often, 1 minute.

5. Stir together eggs in a very large bowl; stir in crumbled cornbread, onion mixture, stuffing mix, pecans, parsley, chicken broth, black pepper, and kosher salt until blended.

6. Spoon mixture into 2 lightly greased 13- x 9-inch (3-qt.) baking dishes. Cover and freeze up to 3 months, if desired; thaw in refrigerator 24 hours. (Uncover and let stand at room temperature 30 minutes before baking.)

7. Bake, uncovered, until lightly browned and cooked through, 1 hour to 1 hour and 15 minutes. Garnish with fresh herb leaves.

Brussels Sprouts with Crunchy Croutons

Toasty brown-butter croutons make simple roasted Brussels sprouts holiday worthy.

SERVES **8 TO 10** ACTIVE **5 MIN.** TOTAL **40 MIN.**

▬

2 lb. Brussels sprouts, trimmed and halved

1½ Tbsp. olive oil

1 tsp. kosher salt

¼ tsp. black pepper

2 cups cubed day-old French bread (½-inch cubes)

¼ cup salted butter

1 shallot, minced

1 Tbsp. fresh thyme leaves

1. Preheat oven to 425°F. Toss together first 4 ingredients in a large bowl; divide evenly between 2 rimmed baking sheets. Bake until golden brown, about 20 minutes. Reduce oven heat to 350°F.

2. Spread bread cubes evenly on a baking sheet; bake at 350°F until browned and crispy, about 15 minutes.

3. Cook butter, stirring constantly, in a medium skillet over medium heat until foaming. Add shallot and thyme; cook, stirring often, 1 minute. Drizzle butter mixture over toasted bread. Arrange sprouts in a serving dish; top with crouton mixture.

Radishes in Warm Herb Butter

Use a colorful mix of Watermelon, French Breakfast, and Easter Egg radishes in this crunchy but warm side. This recipe comes together in minutes, so prep the ingredients in advance and cook it right before serving.

SERVES **8** ACTIVE **10 MIN.** TOTAL **15 MIN.**

▬

1 tsp. fennel seeds

5 Tbsp. cold unsalted butter, diced, divided

1 garlic clove, finely grated

1¾ lb. assorted radishes, trimmed and quartered (about 4 cups)

2 Tbsp. thinly sliced fresh chives

2 Tbsp. finely chopped fresh basil

1½ tsp. coarse gray sea salt

¼ tsp. black pepper

Crush fennel seeds with a rolling pin or heavy skillet. Heat 1 tablespoon of the butter in a large, deep skillet over medium until melted. Stir in crushed fennel seeds and grated garlic; cook, stirring often, until fragrant, about 1 minute. Stir in radishes; cook, stirring constantly, until radishes are warmed through, 2 to 3 minutes. Remove from heat. Add chives, basil, and remaining 4 tablespoons butter; stir until butter is melted. Sprinkle with salt and pepper.

Tasty Swap

These quartered sautèed radishes are a toothsome alternative to the shaved radishes on the Shaved Radish Toasts (page 90).

Butternut Squash Spoonbread

This Southern soufflé likely got its name from suppon or suppawn, an Indian porridge, but the name stuck because this comfort food is best eaten with a spoon. Spoonbread is an any-meal kind of food: Thomas Jefferson is said to have eaten it for breakfast, lunch, and dinner. According to Southern food author, John Egerton, spoonbread is "the ultimate, glorified ideal" of cornbread. "A properly prepared spoonbread," Egerton writes, "can be taken as testimony to the perfectibility of humankind." That's quite an endorsement!

SERVES **8**   ACTIVE **25 MIN.**   TOTAL **1 HOUR, 10 MIN.**

---

2 cups buttermilk

4 large eggs, separated

2 cups thawed, frozen unseasoned, pureed butternut squash

1½ oz. Parmesan cheese, freshly grated (about ⅓ cup)

1 cup stone-ground white cornmeal

1 tsp. baking powder

1 tsp. chopped fresh rosemary, plus more for garnish

½ tsp. baking soda

½ tsp. table salt

¼ cup butter, melted

1. Preheat oven to 350°F. Cook buttermilk in a heavy saucepan over medium-high heat, stirring often, 4 to 6 minutes or until bubbles appear around edges (do not boil); remove from heat. (Mixture may curdle.)

2. Lightly beat egg yolks in a large bowl; stir in squash and cheese. Combine cornmeal and next 4 ingredients in a small bowl. Stir cornmeal mixture into squash mixture. Pour warm buttermilk over squash mixture; whisk until smooth. Let stand 15 minutes or until lukewarm.

3. Brush a 2½- to 3-qt. baking dish or 12-inch cast-iron skillet with 1 Tbsp. melted butter; stir remaining melted butter into squash mixture.

4. Beat egg whites on high speed with an electric mixer until stiff peaks form. Carefully fold into squash mixture. Pour mixture into prepared baking dish.

5. Bake in preheated oven 30 to 35 minutes or until top is golden and a wooden pick inserted in center comes out clean. Garnish with fresh rosemary.

UNDERCOVER FAVORITES

Slow-cooked stews, quickly simmered one-pots, or all-day braises are easy ways to create meals that brim with flavorful complexity. Best of all, they require minimal cleanup, and leftovers taste even better the next day.

Three Sisters Chili

This colorful chili is named for the three companion plants of American Indian agriculture: corn, beans, and squash. It's filling and sneaks better nutrition into a family favorite.

SERVES **8**   ACTIVE **20 MIN.**   TOTAL **55 MIN.**

———

2 (15-oz.) cans red kidney beans, drained and rinsed

2 Tbsp. olive oil

1 medium-size yellow onion, chopped

1 red bell pepper, chopped

2 jalapeño chiles, seeds removed, chopped

3 garlic cloves, minced

1 Tbsp. chili powder

1 Tbsp. kosher salt

½ tsp. ground cumin

½ tsp. smoked paprika

2 lb. butternut squash, peeled, seeds removed, chopped into ½-inch pieces

2 cups frozen corn kernels

1 (15-oz.) can diced tomatoes

4 cups vegetable broth

Chopped fresh flat-leaf parsley

1. Mash ½ cup of the red kidney beans, and set aside with the remaining whole kidney beans.

2. Heat oil in a large stockpot oven over medium. Add onion, bell pepper, jalapeños, and garlic, and cook, stirring often, 5 minutes. Stir in chili powder, salt, cumin, and paprika, and cook, stirring constantly, 1 minute.

3. Increase heat to high; stir in butternut squash, corn, tomatoes, broth, whole beans, and reserved ½ cup mashed beans, and bring to a boil. Reduce heat to medium-low, and simmer, stirring occasionally, until squash is tender, 30 to 45 minutes. Serve sprinkled with parsley.

Stovetop Red Beans & Rice

Make a big batch of this hearty dish for company, or freeze leftovers for later.

MAKES **ABOUT 10 CUPS**   ACTIVE **15 MIN.**
TOTAL **2 HOURS, 45 MIN.**

———

1 lb. dried red kidney beans

½ lb. andouille smoked chicken sausage, thinly sliced

3 celery ribs, chopped

1 green bell pepper, chopped

1 medium onion, chopped

3 garlic cloves, minced

1 Tbsp. Creole seasoning

3 cups uncooked long-grain rice

Sliced scallions

1. Place beans in a Dutch oven; add water 2 inches above beans. Bring to a boil. Boil 1 minute; cover, remove from heat, and soak 1 hour. Drain.

2. Cook sausage and next 3 ingredients in Dutch oven over medium-high 10 minutes or until sausage is browned, stirring often. Add garlic; cook 1 minute. Add beans, Creole seasoning, and 7 cups water. Bring to a boil; reduce heat to low, and simmer 1 to 1½ hours or until beans are tender.

3. Cook rice according to package directions. Serve with red bean mixture. Garnish with scallions.

Tasty Swap

Use this New Orleans staple recipe as a jumping off point for other bean-and-rice dishes. Try these formulas to take the place of the dried beans, sausage, seasoning, and garnish called for here:

Dried cannellini beans + Italian nduja sausage + Italian seasoning + fresh flat-leaf parsley

Dried black beans + Mexican chorizo sausage + adobo seasoning + fresh cilantro

Dried chickpeas + Indian goat sausage + Garam Masala + fresh cilantro

Dried flageolet beans + andouille sausage + herbes de Provence + fresh chervil

Chicken & Shrimp Gumbo

After a day of fasting, a bowl of gumbo on Christmas Eve is a tradition enjoyed by many Louisiana families after midnight church services. One bite of this delicious gumbo might just make it your family's tradition too.

MAKES **10 CUPS.** ACTIVE **45 MIN.**
TOTAL **3 HOURS, 10 MIN., INCLUDING POTATOES**

—

- 1 lb. andouille sausage, cut into ¼-inch-thick slices
- ½ cup peanut oil
- ¾ cup (about 3¼ oz.) all-purpose flour
- 1 large onion, coarsely chopped
- 1 red bell pepper, coarsely chopped
- 1 cup thinly sliced celery
- 2 garlic cloves, minced
- 2 tsp. Cajun seasoning
- ⅛ tsp. cayenne pepper (optional)
- 1 (48-oz.) pkg. chicken broth
- 2 lb. skinned and boned chicken breasts
- ¾ lb. medium-size raw shrimp, peeled and deveined
- Roasted Potatoes (recipe follows)
- Chopped fresh flat-leaf parsley, sliced scallion, hot sauce

1. Cook sausage in a large skillet over medium, stirring often, 7 minutes or until browned. Remove sausage; drain and pat dry with paper towels.

2. Heat oil in a stainless-steel Dutch oven over medium; gradually whisk in flour, and cook, whisking constantly, 18 to 20 minutes or until flour is caramel color. (Do not burn mixture.) Reduce heat to low, and cook, whisking constantly, until mixture is milk chocolate-color and texture is smooth (about 2 minutes).

3. Increase heat to medium. Stir in onion, next 4 ingredients, and, if desired, cayenne pepper. Cook, stirring constantly, 3 minutes. Gradually stir in chicken broth; add chicken and sausage. Increase heat to medium-high, and bring to a boil. Reduce heat to low, and simmer, stirring occasionally, 1 hour and 30 minutes to 1 hour and 40 minutes or until chicken is done. Shred chicken into large pieces using 2 forks. Add shrimp; cook 5 minutes more.

4. Place Roasted Potatoes in serving bowls. Spoon gumbo over potatoes. Serve immediately with desired toppings.

Roasted Potatoes

- 3 lb. baby red potatoes, quartered
- 1 Tbsp. peanut oil
- 1 tsp. kosher salt

Preheat oven to 450°F. Stir together all ingredients in a large bowl. Place potatoes in a single layer in a lightly greased 15- x 10-inch jelly-roll pan. Bake 40 to 45 minutes or until tender and browned, stirring twice. MAKES ABOUT 10 CUPS

Chicken Thighs with Parsnips & Oranges

You'll love the earthy sweetness of this easy braise. Serve over rice or mashed potatoes

SERVES **4** ACTIVE **10 MIN.** TOTAL **45 MIN.**

—

- 8 bone-in, skin-on chicken thighs, trimmed (about 3 lb.)
- 2 tsp. paprika
- 1 tsp. kosher salt, divided
- 1 tsp. black pepper, divided
- 2 Tbsp. salted butter
- 1 lb. large parsnips, halved lengthwise and cut into 1½-inch-long pieces
- 2½ Tbsp. all-purpose flour
- 2 cups chicken broth
- 4 oregano sprigs
- 1 small orange, sliced
- 3 cups hot cooked mashed potatoes or rice (optional)
- Fresh thyme leaves

1. Pat chicken dry with paper towels. Sprinkle chicken with paprika and ¾ teaspoon each of the salt and black pepper. Melt butter in a large enamel-coated cast-iron skillet with lid over medium-high. Place half of chicken, skin-side down, in skillet; cook until skin is golden brown, about 6 minutes. Remove chicken from skillet; repeat process with remaining chicken.

2. Add parsnips to pan. Cook, stirring occasionally, until browned, about 7 minutes. Add flour; cook, stirring often, 1 minute. Add broth, oregano, and remaining ¼ teaspoon salt and black pepper; bring to a boil. Place chicken, skin-side up, on parsnips. Partially cover; reduce heat to medium-low. Cook until chicken is 170°F, about 20 minutes. Remove thyme sprigs. Stir in oranges. Serve over mashed potatoes, if desired. Garnish with thyme leaves.

Saffron Veal Stew

The late entertaining expert Julia Reed served this stew over noodles, rice, or potato puree.

SERVES **8**   ACTIVE **50 MIN.**   TOTAL **1 HOUR, 40 MIN.**

—

4 lb. veal stew meat, cut into 2-inch pieces

3½ tsp. kosher salt, divided

1½ tsp. black pepper, divided

3 Tbsp. all-purpose flour

¼ cup olive oil, divided

1 cup dry white wine

2 leeks

1 large onion, halved and studded with 2 whole cloves

2 carrots, quartered

2 celery stalks, roughly chopped

4 garlic cloves, sliced

1 lemon, peel removed in strips with a vegetable peeler

2 bay leaves

2 fresh thyme sprigs

4 cups chicken broth, divided

1 tsp. saffron threads

1 cup peeled pearl onions

3 Tbsp. (1½ oz.) salted butter, divided

2 (8-oz.) pkg. button mushrooms

1 cup crème fraîche

3 Tbsp. grated Parmesan cheese

3 Tbsp. minced fresh chives

1 Tbsp. chopped fresh tarragon leaves

1. Sprinkle veal with 2 teaspoons salt and 1 teaspoon black pepper; sprinkle with flour, and toss to coat.

2. Heat 2 tablespoons oil in a large Dutch oven over high. Add veal, and cook, in batches if necessary, until browned on all sides, 5 to 6 minutes. Transfer veal to a paper towel-lined sheet pan. Add wine to Dutch oven, and stir, scraping up any browned bits from bottom of pot. Reduce heat to medium, and simmer until wine is reduced by half.

3. Cut and discard root ends and dark green tops from leeks, reserving white and pale-green parts only. Cut into 1-inch pieces, and rinse thoroughly.

4. Return veal to Dutch oven. Add leeks and next 7 ingredients, and cook, stirring often, until vegetables begin to soften, 8 to 10 minutes. Stir in 3 cups broth and bring to a boil over high. Reduce heat to low, add saffron, and cover. Simmer until meat is tender, about 1 hour.

5. Meanwhile, bring remaining 1 cup broth to a boil in a saucepan. Add onions, 1 tablespoon butter, and ½ teaspoon salt. Reduce heat to low; cover and simmer until onions are tender, about 10 minutes. Drain over a small bowl, reserving onion liquid. Set cooked onions aside.

6. Melt remaining 2 tablespoons butter with remaining 2 tablespoons oil in a large skillet over high. Add mushrooms; sprinkle with remaining 1 teaspoon salt and ½ teaspoon black pepper. Cook, stirring often, until mushrooms are browned, about 5 minutes. Remove from heat.

7. Pour veal mixture in Dutch oven through a colander into a large bowl. Remove veal pieces, and reserve; discard vegetables. Transfer veal sauce in bowl to Dutch oven, and bring to a boil over high. Reduce heat to medium, and cook 5 minutes, stirring occasionally. Whisk in crème fraîche and Parmesan until blended and smooth, adding desired amount of reserved onion liquid if sauce is too thick. Stir in cooked veal, pearl onions, and mushrooms. Stir in chives and tarragon.

Tasty Swap

For an inexpensive veal swap, substitute beef chuck or shoulder for the veal. You can also use pork shoulder or Boston Butt here.

TINY TEMPTATIONS

Sweet treats are a favorite indulgence of the holiday season. Whether fruity, frosted, crunchy or gooey, these are perfectly portioned for enjoying now or sharing with others.

Mighty Mint Pinwheels

Kids love these swirly, not-too-minty cookies.

MAKES **ABOUT 5 DOZEN**   ACTIVE **30 MIN.**
TOTAL **4 HOURS**

—

1 cup salted butter, softened

1½ cups granulated sugar

1 large egg

1 tsp. mint extract

1 tsp. vanilla extract

2½ cups (about 10½ oz.) all-purpose flour

1½ tsp. baking powder

¼ tsp. table salt

Green and/or red food coloring paste or gel

1. Beat butter with a heavy-duty stand mixer on medium speed until creamy, about 2 minutes; gradually add sugar, beating well. Add egg and extracts, beating until combined.

2. Stir together flour, baking powder, and salt in a small bowl. Gradually add to butter mixture, beating on low speed just until blended.

3. Divide dough in half; add desired amount of green or red food coloring to 1 portion, and knead until color is distributed. Shape dough halves into disks; wrap in plastic wrap, and chill until firm, about 1 hour.

4. Divide each half of dough into 2 equal portions. Roll out each portion on floured wax paper into an 8-inch square, trimming edges if necessary.

5. Invert 1 uncolored dough square onto 1 colored dough square; peel wax paper from white dough. Tightly roll up dough, jelly-roll fashion, peeling wax paper from colored dough as you roll. Repeat with remaining dough squares. Wrap rolls in plastic wrap, and chill 2 hours.

6. Preheat oven to 350°F. Remove dough from refrigerator, and cut into ¼-inch-thick slices; place slices 2 inches apart on parchment paper-lined baking sheets. (Keep unbaked dough chilled while baking cookies.)

7. Bake, in batches, in preheated oven until bottoms are lightly browned, 10 to 12 minutes. Remove cookies from pans to wire racks, and cool completely.

Peppermint Pinwheels

Prepare recipe as directed, substitute peppermint extract for the mint extract and red food coloring paste or gel for the green.

Raspberry Palmiers

You'd never guess these impressive-looking cookies are made with just four ingredients.

MAKES **ABOUT 31/2 DOZEN**   ACTIVE **20 MIN.**
TOTAL **1 HOUR, 25 MIN.**

—

¾ cup Demerara sugar

1 tsp. ground cinnamon

1 (17.3-oz.) pkg. frozen puff pastry sheets, thawed

⅔ cup raspberry jam

1. Combine sugar and cinnamon in a small bowl. Sprinkle ¼ cup sugar mixture over a 12-inch square on a work surface. Unfold 1 pastry sheet on top of sugar, and roll sheet into a 12- x 9-inch rectangle. Spread ⅓ cup jam over dough, leaving a ½-inch border around edges. Starting with 1 long side, roll up pastry, jelly-roll fashion, to center of pastry sheet. Roll opposite side to center. (The shape will resemble a scroll.) Wrap in plastic wrap, and freeze 20 minutes. Repeat procedure with ¼ cup of the sugar mixture and remaining pastry sheet and ⅓ cup jam.

2. Preheat oven to 375°F. Remove 1 pastry roll from freezer, and cut into ½-inch-thick slices; place 2 inches apart on a parchment paper-lined baking sheet. Sprinkle each slice with a small amount of the remaining sugar mixture.

3. Bake in preheated oven until light golden brown on the bottom, 14 to 16 minutes. Remove from oven, and carefully turn each cookie over. Return to oven, and bake until crisp and golden brown, 8 to 10 more minutes. Transfer cookies to a wire rack, and cool completely, about 30 minutes. Repeat procedure with the remaining pastry roll.

Mocha-Mint Sablés

"Sablé" means "sandy" and these French sugar cookies have a shortbread-like texture with loads of chocolate flavor.

MAKES **ABOUT 4½ DOZEN**   ACTIVE **20 MIN.**
TOTAL **1 HOUR, 40 MIN.**

———

1 cup salted butter, softened

1 cup powdered sugar

1 tsp. vanilla extract

2 cups (about 8½ oz.) all-purpose flour

¼ cup unsweetened cocoa

1 Tbsp. instant espresso powder

½ tsp. kosher salt

2½ (4-oz.) 60% cacao bittersweet chocolate baking bars

20 small peppermint candies, crushed

1. Beat butter and sugar with an electric mixer on medium speed until creamy; add vanilla, and beat until combined. Stir together flour, cocoa, espresso powder, and salt. Gradually add flour mixture to butter mixture, beating at low speed until combined after each addition. Finely chop 1 of the bittersweet chocolate baking bars, and stir into cookie dough until well incorporated.

2. Divide dough in half; shape each into an 8-inch-long log. Wrap each log tightly in plastic wrap, and freeze until firm, about 30 minutes. (Dough may be frozen up to 1 month.)

3. Preheat oven to 350°F. Cut dough into ¼-inch-thick slices, and place 2 inches apart on parchment paper-lined baking sheets. (Keep dough logs refrigerated while cookies bake. Bake until bottoms are lightly browned, 11 to 13 minutes. Cool on pans 5 minutes; remove cookies to wire racks, and cool completely, about 20 minutes.

4. Chop remaining 1½ bittersweet chocolate baking bars, and place in a small microwavable bowl. Microwave on HIGH until chocolate is melted and smooth, 1 to 1½ minutes, stirring every 30 seconds.

5. Dip half of top side of each cookie in melted chocolate. Sprinkle lightly with crushed peppermints. Place cookies on a parchment paper-lined baking sheet, and chill just until chocolate sets, about 15 minutes. Layer cookies between wax paper, and store in an airtight container at room temperature up to 5 days.

Fruit-and-Nut Icebox Cookies

With its fun stripes and surprising combination of apricot preserves and salted pistachios, this is a stand-out cookie recipe with countless variations. See the "Tasty Swap" sidebar on the following page for a handful of ideas for worthy flavor combinations. Double this recipe so that your family can enjoy a batch and you can package up the rest to share.

MAKES **2 DOZEN**   ACTIVE **30 MIN.**
TOTAL **2 HOURS, 30 MIN.**

———

½ cup salted butter, softened

1 cup granulated sugar

1 large egg

1 tsp. vanilla extract

1¾ cups (about 7½ oz.) all-purpose flour

1 tsp. baking powder

¼ tsp. table salt

½ cup apricot preserves

½ cup finely chopped roasted salted pistachios

1. Cut parchment paper into 8 (12- x 6-inch) rectangles. Beat butter with a heavy-duty stand mixer on medium speed until creamy, about 2 minutes; add sugar, and beat until light and fluffy, about 3 minutes. Add egg and vanilla, and beat until combined.

2. Stir together flour, baking powder, and salt in a small bowl. Gradually add flour mixture to butter mixture, beating on low speed until blended.

3. Transfer dough to work surface; divide into 4 equal portions. Place 1 dough portion between 2 parchment rectangles. Roll out to a 9- x 3½-inch rectangle about ¼ inch thick. Repeat with remaining dough. Place dough (between parchment paper) on a baking sheet; freeze 30 minutes.

4. Pulse apricot preserves in a food processor until large pieces are broken apart.

5. Remove dough from freezer. Remove top pieces of parchment from the dough Spread 2½ tablespoons of the preserves over 1 dough rectangle. Sprinkle with about 8 teaspoons of the finely chopped pistachios. Top with 1 dough rectangle. Repeat with remaining preserves, pistachios, and dough rectangles, leaving the top rectangle uncoated. Trim dough stack to an 8½- x 3¼-inch brick. Wrap dough in plastic wrap, and freeze 1 hour.

6. Preheat oven to 350°F. Remove dough from freezer, and slice into ¼-inch-thick rectangles; place on parchment paper-lined baking sheets.

7. Bake in preheated oven until lightly browned around edges, 13 to 15 minutes. Cool on baking sheets 5 minutes. Transfer to wire racks, and cool completely, about 20 minutes.

Tasty Swap

Prepare the Fruit-and-Nut Icebox Cookies recipe as directed, but change up the fruit and nut combination to suit your tastes. Below are some flavorful combos worth baking up:

- apple butter + walnuts
- blueberry jam + sunflower kernels
- fig preserves + pine nuts
- grape jelly + peanuts
- lemon curd + cashews
- orange marmalade + sesame seeds
- peach preserves + pecans
- pepper jelly + pepitas
- pineapple preserves + macadamia nuts
- raspberry preserves + almonds
- red currant jelly + hazelnuts
- strawberry preserves + pistachios

Cookie Know-How

Butter and eggs should always be at room temperature in order for ingredients to blend properly.

Butter should be soft to the touch, not melted, unless otherwise directed in the recipe. Use regular butter for best results. Soft-style tub butter has higher moisture and air content, which can affect cookies and other baked goods.

All of these cookie recipes call for all-purpose flour. Do not substitute another type of flour, such as cake or self-rising flour, because they react differently and will not yield the anticipated final product.

Use shiny baking sheets. We find that dark, nonstick pans generally yield a darker cookie because they absorb more heat. Allow baking sheets to cool in between batches to prevent cookie dough from melting upon contact with the hot pan.

Always cool cookies completely before storing. Use airtight containers for chewy cookies and tins or jars for crispy cookies.

Some cookies are excellent candidates for freezing. Place cookies in layers on wax paper in airtight containers; for absolute freshness, freeze up to 1 month. Thaw frozen cookies at room temperature 10 to 15 minutes before serving.

Box Mix Cupcakes with Brown Butter Frosting

Decadent, nutty homemade frosting elevates this cake made from a boxed mix for an almost from-scratch gift anyone would be delighted to receive.

MAKES **24 CUPCAKES**   ACTIVE **20 MIN.**
TOTAL **1 HOUR, 45 MIN., INCLUDING FROSTING**

1 (16-oz.) pkg. pound cake mix

Browned Butter Frosting (recipe follows)

Chopped toasted pecans

1. Preheat oven to 350°F. Prepare pound cake mix according to package directions. Place 24 paper baking cups in muffin pans; spoon batter evenly into paper cups, filling two-thirds full.

2. Bake in preheated oven until a wooden pick inserted in center of cupcake comes out clean, about 20 minutes. Remove cupcakes from pan, and let cool completely on wire racks.

3. Spread cupcakes evenly with Brown Butter Frosting; garnish with chopped toasted pecans.

Brown Butter Frosting

1 cup butter

1 (16-oz.) pkg. powdered sugar

¼ cup milk

1 tsp. vanilla extract

1. Cook butter in a small heavy saucepan over medium, stirring constantly, 6 to 8 minutes or until butter begins to turn golden brown. Remove pan from heat immediately, and pour butter into small bowl. Cover and chill 1 hour or until butter is cool and begins to solidify.

2. Beat butter on medium speed with an electric mixer until fluffy; gradually add powdered sugar alternately with milk, beginning and ending with powdered sugar. Beat on low speed until well blended after each addition. Stir in vanilla.
MAKES ABOUT 3½ CUPS

Snowy Chocolate Baby Cakes

Festive and fun, there is no need to feel guilty if you eat more than one!

MAKES **24 CAKES**   ACTIVE **45 MIN.**
TOTAL **1 HOUR, 50 MIN., INCLUDING GLAZE**

1 (18.25-oz.) pkg. devil's food cake mix

1 (16-oz.) container sour cream

½ cup milk

¼ cup butter, melted

2 large eggs

1 tsp. vanilla extract

Winter White Glaze (recipe follows)

Red cinnamon candies, fresh mint leaves

1. Preheat oven to 350°F. Beat first 6 ingredients on low speed with an electric mixer just until dry ingredients are moistened. Increase speed to medium, and beat 1 to 2 minutes or until smooth, stopping to scrape bowl as needed. Spoon batter into 2 greased and floured (12-cup) muffin pans.

2. Bake in preheated oven until a wooden pick inserted in centers comes out clean, 20 to 22 minutes or. Cool in pans 5 minutes. Remove from pans to wire racks, and cool completely (about 30 minutes).

3. Arrange cakes upside down on a serving platter. Spoon Winter White Glaze over cakes (about 1 Tbsp. per cake), spreading with a spatula to thoroughly cover cakes. Garnish with candies and mint leaves.

Winter White Glaze

4 cups powdered sugar

1 Tbsp. meringue powder

¼ cup hot water

Beat together all ingredients with an electric mixer until smooth. Use immediately. (Cover glaze surface directly with a damp paper towel, as needed, to prevent a crust from forming before you've finished icing the cupcakes.) MAKES ABOUT 2 CUPS

Molten Red Velvet Cakes

Sharing dessert is overrated. These single-serving molten cakes are a sweet
way to end a festive meal. The chocolate mixture and frosting can be made
1 day in advance, and the cakes take less than 20 minutes to bake.

MAKES **4 CAKES**   ACTIVE **20 MIN.**   TOTAL **2 HOURS, 35 MIN.**

CAKES

2 oz. semisweet chocolate baking bar, finely chopped

¼ cup heavy cream

1 cup (about 3¾ oz.) cake flour

1½ tsp. unsweetened cocoa, plus more for ramekins

¼ tsp. baking soda

¼ tsp. table salt

½ cup salted butter, melted, plus more for ramekins

½ cup granulated sugar

6 Tbsp. buttermilk

1½ tsp. red liquid food coloring

½ tsp. vanilla extract

½ tsp. apple cider vinegar

1 large egg yolk

CREAM CHEESE WHIPPED CREAM

2 oz. cream cheese, softened

3 Tbsp. powdered sugar

½ tsp. vanilla extract

¾ cup heavy cream

ADDITIONAL INGREDIENT

1 Tbsp. powdered sugar

1. Prepare the Cakes: Combine chopped semisweet chocolate and heavy cream in a small microwavable bowl. Microwave on high 30 seconds. Let stand 1 minute; whisk until melted and smooth. Place plastic wrap directly on chocolate mixture (to prevent a skin from forming); chill until firm, about 2 hours. Chocolate mixture can be prepared 1 day in advance; store, covered, in the refrigerator.

2. Preheat oven to 400°F. Grease 4 (8-ounce) ramekins with butter; dust with unsweetened cocoa, and tap out excess. Whisk together flour, cocoa, baking soda, and salt in a medium bowl. Whisk together melted butter, granulated sugar, buttermilk, food coloring, vanilla, vinegar, and egg yolk in a separate bowl. Add butter mixture to flour mixture, and whisk just until blended. Divide batter evenly among prepared ramekins.

3. Using a small (1¼- or 1½-inch) cookie scoop, portion chilled chocolate mixture into 4 balls. Place 1 chocolate ball in center of batter in each ramekin, pressing lightly. (Chocolate will sink into batter as it bakes.) Place ramekins on a baking sheet. Bake in preheated oven until center springs back when lightly pressed, about 18 minutes.

4. Meanwhile, prepare the Cream Cheese Whipped Cream: Stir together cream cheese, powdered sugar, and vanilla in a medium bowl until smooth. Add heavy cream; beat with an electric mixer at medium-high speed until soft peaks form, 30 seconds to 1 minute, scraping down sides of bowl as needed.

5. Remove cakes from oven. Immediately run an offset spatula or thin knife around outer edge of cakes to loosen; invert each cake onto a serving plate. Dust the cakes evenly with 1 Tbsp. powdered sugar. Top cakes with Cream Cheese Whipped Cream, and serve immediately.

Mini Bourbon-&-Cheerwine Bundt Cakes

North Carolina's beloved Cheerwine pairs well with bourbon and is a terrific stand-in for the more common cola in these super-moist baby bundts.

MAKES **3 DOZEN**   ACTIVE **20 MIN.**
TOTAL **1 HOUR, 40 MIN., INCLUDING GLAZE**

—

1½ cups butter, softened

2½ cups granulated sugar

3 large eggs

1½ tsp. vanilla extract

1 cup Cheerwine soft drink

¾ cup buttermilk

½ cup bourbon

3 cups (about 12¾ oz.) all-purpose flour

½ cup unsweetened cocoa

½ tsp. baking soda

½ tsp. table salt

Bourbon-&-Cheerwine Glaze

Powdered sugar, optional

1. Preheat oven to 350°F. Beat butter on medium speed with an electric mixer until creamy. Gradually add sugar; beat until blended. Add eggs and vanilla; beat on low speed until blended.

2. Stir together Cheerwine and next 2 ingredients in a small bowl. Combine flour and next 3 ingredients in another bowl. Add flour mixture to butter mixture alternately with Cheerwine mixture, beginning and ending with flour mixture. Beat on low speed just until blended after each addition, stopping to scrape bowl as needed. Pour batter into 3 lightly greased 12-cup Bundt brownie pans, filling each three-fourths full.

3. Bake in preheated oven until a wooden pick inserted in center comes out clean, 12 to 15 minutes. Cool in pan on a wire rack 10 minutes. Remove from pans to wire racks, and cool 30 minutes. Drizzle warm glaze over cakes. Dust with powdered sugar.

Bourbon-&-Cheerwine Glaze

¼ cup butter

3 Tbsp. Cheerwine soft drink

2½ Tbsp. unsweetened cocoa

1 Tbsp. bourbon

2 cups plus 2 Tbsp. powdered sugar

Cook first 3 ingredients in a saucepan over medium-low, stirring constantly. Remove from heat; stir in bourbon. Beat in powdered sugar with an electric mixer. MAKES ABOUT 1 CUP

TEST KITCHEN TIP: We love adding soft drinks to our cakes and glazes for the unique sweet flavors that they impart, yet they do more than add a distinctive flavor note. Their addition keeps cakes moist and delightfully airy. The carbonation acts as a leavening agent to help the cake rise in the oven. So whether you like vanilla or chocolate, layer cakes or sheet cakes, consider adding some soda fountain bubbly in place of the usual liquid called for in your recipe. Sip the rest while the cake bakes.

RISE & BRINE

Warm yeasty breads and crunchy mouthwatering pickles are irresistible gifts from the kitchen guaranteed to make friends and family smile. Wrap these food gifts up creatively and be sure to include a recipe card so that the recipient can make it again.

Christmas Morning Orange Rolls

Orange rolls are to Christmas morning what dressing is to the Thanksgiving table—
a standard. Sour cream gives these an extra tender crumb while a mix of orange zest
and juice really boosts the citrus flavor.

MAKES **1 DOZEN**   ACTIVE **35 MIN.**   TOTAL **1 HOUR, PLUS 2 HOURS, 15 MIN., INCLUDING RISING TIME**

▬

**3¾ cups (about 16 oz.)
  all-purpose flour, plus more
  for work surface**

½ cup whole milk

½ cup sour cream

6 Tbsp. unsalted butter, melted

2 tsp. kosher salt

1 large egg, lightly beaten

**1 (¼-oz.) envelope instant or
  quick-rising yeast (such as
  Fleischmann's RapidRise)**

1 cup granulated sugar, divided

½ cup unsalted butter, softened

**2 Tbsp., plus 1 tsp. orange zest,
  divided, and 3 to 4 Tbsp. juice**

2 cups powdered sugar

1. Combine flour, milk, sour cream, melted butter, salt, egg, yeast, and ⅓ cup of the granulated sugar in bowl of a stand mixer fitted with paddle attachment. Beat on medium speed until dough forms, 1 minute. Turn off mixer. Switch to dough hook attachment. Beat on medium speed until dough is smooth and elastic, about 6 minutes. (Dough should pull away from sides of bowl but stick to bottom.)

2. Spray a large bowl with cooking spray. Place dough in bowl, turning to coat all sides. Cover and let rise in a warm, draft-free place (about 75°F) until dough has doubled in size, about 1 hour and 30 minutes.

3. Lightly punch down dough. Roll dough out on a lightly floured surface into a 19- x 13-inch rectangle. Spread softened butter over dough.

4. Stir together 3 tablespoons of the orange zest and remaining ⅔ cup granulated sugar. Sprinkle sugar mixture over buttered dough, gently pressing to adhere. Starting with 1 long side, roll dough into a log, and pinch seam to seal. Turn log seam-side down, and cut into 12 rolls.

5. Spray a 12-cup muffin pan with cooking spray. Using your thumb, push upward slightly beneath bottom center of each roll, and place rolls into prepared pan. Cover with plastic wrap, and let rise in a warm, draft-free place (about 75°F) until almost doubled in size, 45 minutes.

6. Preheat oven to 350°F. Uncover rolls. Bake until golden brown and cooked through, about 20 minutes. Transfer pan to a wire rack; let stand in pan 5 minutes. Remove rolls to wire rack.

7. Whisk together powdered sugar, 3 tablespoons of the orange juice, and remaining 1 teaspoon orange zest in a bowl, adding remaining 1 tablespoon juice 1 teaspoon at a time, if needed, for desired consistency. Drizzle glaze over warm rolls.

SAVOR & SHARE

Cranberry Pull-Apart Bread with Orange-Cream Cheese Icing

The entire family will love the sticky-fingered fun of tearing apart these sweet layers filled with tangy cranberries and bright orange zest. The recipe makes two loaves of bread; give one as a gift, and take the other to brunch.

MAKES **2 LOAVES**   ACTIVE **40 MIN.**   TOTAL **3 HOURS, 15 MIN.**

—

BREAD

¼ cup warm water
(100°F to 110°F)

1 (¼-oz.) envelope active dry yeast

¾ cup plus 1 tsp. granulated sugar, divided

¼ cup unsalted butter, softened

1 tsp. table salt

2 large eggs

1 cup whole milk

4½ to 5 cups (about 21 oz.) bread flour, divided, plus more for dusting

1½ cups frozen cranberries (about 51/2 oz.), thawed and coarsely chopped

1 Tbsp. orange zest (from 1 orange)

ICING

2 oz. cream cheese, softened

2 Tbsp. unsalted butter, softened

⅛ tsp. table salt

2¼ cups (about 9 oz.) powdered sugar

1 tsp. vanilla extract

2 Tbsp. fresh orange juice, divided (from 1 orange)

1. Prepare the Bread: Stir together warm water, active dry yeast, and 1 teaspoon of the granulated sugar in a small bowl. Let stand until foamy, about 5 minutes.

2. Beat butter with a heavy-duty electric stand mixer on medium speed until creamy, about 1 minute. Add salt and ½ cup of the granulated sugar; beat until light and fluffy, about 3 minutes. Add eggs, 1 at a time, beating well after each addition. Stir in whole milk and yeast mixture. Gradually add 4½ cups of the bread flour, beating on medium-low just until combined.

3. Turn dough out onto a lightly floured work surface. Knead until smooth and elastic, about 5 minutes, adding up to ½ cup flour in very small amounts, if necessary to keep dough workable. Place dough in a lightly greased bowl, turning to coat all sides. Cover and let stand in a warm place until dough doubles in size, about 1 hour and 30 minutes.

4. Combine frozen cranberries, orange zest, and remaining ¼ cup granulated sugar in a medium bowl. Set aside.

5. Turn dough out onto a lightly floured work surface. Divide dough in half. Roll 1 dough half into a 16- x 10-inch rectangle, and cut into 8 (5- x 4-inch) rectangles. Spoon about 1 tablespoon of the cranberry mixture onto each rectangle. Fold rectangles in half over filling so that short sides meet. Then stand, cut side up and folded side down, in a lightly greased 8- x 4-inch loaf pan. Repeat with second dough half and remaining cranberry mixture in a second loaf pan. Cover pans loosely with plastic wrap, and let stand in a warm place until dough doubles in size, about 1 hour.

6. Preheat oven to 350°F. Remove and discard plastic wrap. Bake until golden brown and a wooden skewer inserted in center comes out clean, about 30 minutes, shielding with aluminum foil after 20 minutes to prevent excess browning, if necessary.

7. Cool in pans 10 minutes. Transfer from pans to wire rack to cool slightly, at least 10 minutes.

8. Prepare the Icing: While bread cools, beat cream cheese, butter, and salt with an electric mixer on medium speed until creamy. Gradually add powdered sugar, beating until combined. Stir in vanilla extract and 1 tablespoon of the orange juice. Stir in up to 1 more tablespoon orange juice, 1 teaspoon at a time, until it's smooth and creamy.

9. Drizzle bread lightly with Icing, and serve with remaining Icing on the side for dipping.

Sally Lunn

The no-knead recipe came from England, but Southerners have been starry-eyed for the brioche-like loaf for decades.

SERVES **8 TO 10**   ACTIVE **15 MIN.**   TOTAL **2 HOURS**

1 cup warm milk
   (100°F to 110°F)

1 (¼-oz.) envelope active
   dry yeast

1 tsp. granulated sugar

4 cups (about 17 oz.)
   all-purpose flour

¼ to ½ cup granulated
   sugar

1 tsp. table salt

3 large eggs, lightly
   beaten

½ cup warm water
   (100°F to 110°F)

½ tsp. baking soda

½ cup butter, melted

Fruit Butter (recipe
   follows)

1. Stir together first 3 ingredients in a 2-cup glass measuring cup; let stand 5 minutes.

2. Stir together flour and next 2 ingredients in a large bowl. Stir in eggs until well blended. (Dough will look shaggy.) Stir together warm water and baking soda. Stir yeast mixture, soda mixture, and melted butter into flour mixture until well blended.

3. Spoon batter into a well-greased 10-inch (14-cup) tube pan. Cover with plastic wrap, and let rise in a warm place (80°F to 85°F), 45 minutes to 1 hour or until doubled in bulk.

4. Preheat oven to 400°F. Carefully place pan in oven. (Do not agitate dough.) Bake 25 to 30 minutes or until a wooden pick inserted in center comes out clean. Remove from pan to a wire rack, and cool 30 minutes before slicing. Serve with Fruit Butter, if desired.

Fruit Butter

Blend 2 to 3 tablespoons seedless jam into ½ cup softened unsalted butter.

Conquer the Rise

Don't be intimidated by yeast; embrace it. A friendly fungus, yeast is microscopic magic that leavens bread and gives it a unique texture and flavor. You'll find instant (or "rapid-rise") and active dry yeast. We recommend active dry—the activation (Step 2, below) means the yeast is alive and ready to go to work. Follow our steps, and your bread will rise to the occasion.

STEP 1: STORE Use yeast packets before the expiration date. To store yeast after it has been opened, refrigerate the granules in an airtight container.

STEP 2: ACTIVATE Stir active dry yeast into warm water (100°F to 110°F). If it's too cold, the granules will remain dormant; if it's too hot, the yeast will die. Yeast loves sugar, so add a pinch to speed up activation (aka "proofing"). If bubbles appear, you're golden. That's the gas that makes bread rise.

STEP 3: MIX Mix the bubbly brew with flour to make a shaggy dough. Most recipes call for a pinch of salt, not just for flavor but also to slow the activation process, keeping the yeast in check so it doesn't activate too quickly.

STEP 4: KNEAD Knead the dough to create gluten, which behaves like bubble gum. It traps tiny gas bubbles produced by the yeast and stretches to give bread its springy texture.

STEP 5: RISE Bubbles multiply and grow as the yeast starts fermenting, which gives bread its unique flavor and texture. After this first rise, shape the dough, let it rise again briefly, and bake it!

Pickled Pearl Onions

These easy refrigerator onions don't require a hot water bath. Be sure to label jars
with their contents, packing date, and how long it keeps (one month for these).

MAKES **1 QUART**   ACTIVE **10 MIN.**   TOTAL **20 MIN.**

1¼ cups apple cider vinegar

1¼ cups water

2 Tbsp. granulated sugar

1½ Tbsp. pickling salt

6 dried allspice berries

6 black peppercorns

1 whole clove

3 (10-oz.) pkg. fresh pearl onions,
   peeled according to package
   directions

1. Combine vinegar, water, sugar, pickling salt, allspice berries, peppercorns, and clove in a nonreactive saucepan; bring to a boil over high. Add onions; reduce heat to low, and simmer 5 minutes.

2. Transfer onions into 1 (1-quart) canning jar or 2 (1-pint) canning jars with a slotted spoon, leaving ½ inch of room at the top, reserving liquid in saucepan.

3. Carefully ladle hot vinegar mixture over onions in jars, leaving ½ inch of room at the top of each. Discard any remaining liquid. Wipe jar rims. Cover at once with metal lids; screw on bands. Cool jars to room temperature. Onions will keep up to 1 month in refrigerator.

TEST KITCHEN TIP: To eliminate potentially dangerous microbes in food, it's important to follow brine ratios and cook times. Pickled vegetables and fruit, like this recipe and the three that follow, will keep in the refrigerator one to three months, unless they have garlic or oil in them, in which case their lifespan goes down to about one week. You can find the guidelines set by the National Center for Home Food Preservation at nchfp.uga.edu.

SAVOR & SHARE

Fiery Pickled Carrots

These quick-pickled carrots are a nice cool season-change of pace on the Bloody Mary bar. Enjoy them chopped on a barbecue sandwich in place of chow chow or the usual dill pickles.

SERVES **10**   ACTIVE **10 MIN.**
TOTAL **4 HOURS, 10 MIN.**

---

1 lb. small carrots, trimmed

1½ cups white vinegar

¼ cup granulated sugar

1½ tsp. kosher salt

1 tsp. onion powder

1 tsp. crushed red pepper

½ tsp. mustard seeds

1. Place carrots in a medium saucepan with water to cover, and bring to a boil over high. Reduce heat to medium, and simmer just until tender, 8 to 10 minutes. Drain and rinse with cold water; drain completely, and place in a large bowl.

2. Stir together white vinegar, 1 cup water, sugar, salt, onion powder, crushed red pepper, and mustard seeds in a medium saucepan. Bring to a boil over medium-high, stirring to dissolve sugar and salt. Pour hot liquid over carrots; cover and chill at least 4 hours or up to overnight. Carrots will keep chilled up to 1 month in the refrigerator.

Quick-Pickled Beets

Another cool-season crop perfect for pickling, try this recipe with yellow or orange beets, too. Enjoy them on a relish tray or in salads.

SERVES **10**   ACTIVE **20 MIN.**   TOTAL **5 HOURS**

1½ lb. small red beets

1 cup apple cider vinegar

½ cup granulated sugar

½ cup thinly sliced red onion

2 tsp. dried thyme

1 tsp. kosher salt

1 tsp. dried oregano

1 tsp. black peppercorns

1. Trim ends of beets, leaving roots and 1-inch stems; scrub with a brush. Place in a medium saucepan with water to cover; bring to a boil over high. Cover, reduce heat to medium, and simmer until tender, about 45 minutes. Drain and rinse with cold water, and drain completely. Cool 5 minutes. Trim roots, and rub off skins.

2. Cut beets into ¼-inch-thick slices, and place in a large bowl. Stir together apple cider vinegar and 1 cup water in a medium saucepan. Add the sugar, onion, thyme, salt, dried oregano, and peppercorns. Bring to a boil over medium-high, stirring to dissolve sugar and salt. Pour hot liquid over beets; cover and chill at least 4 hours or up to overnight. Beets will keep up to 1 month chilled in the refrigerator.

Pickled Grapes

These grapes are a tasty sweet-tart addition to a cheese and charcuterie board...not to mention that they make a terrific hostess gift.

MAKES **4 CUPS**   ACTIVE **10 MIN.**   TOTAL **3 DAYS, INCLUDING CHILLING TIME**

---

1 lb. green or red seedless grapes, preferably small

3 star anise pods

6 whole allspice

1 cup apple cider vinegar

1 cup granulated sugar

1 Tbsp. whole black peppercorns

1 tsp. yellow mustard seeds

1 tsp. fennel seeds

¼ tsp. table salt

1. Rinse grapes and snip into small clusters, leaving stems attached. Pack grapes and star anise pods into a 1-qt. heat-resistant glass measuring cup or a wide-mouthed jar.

2. Combine remaining ingredients in a medium saucepan over high heat; bring to a boil. Cook until sugar dissolves; remove from heat and pour hot liquid over grapes. Let cool, then set a small saucer on top and a weight, as needed, to keep grapes immersed. Chill 2 to 3 days, depending on size (larger grapes take longer to pickle). Keep chilled and enjoy within 2 weeks.

TEST KITCHEN TIP: We love a charcuterie board! It's guaranteed to draw any crowd to the table. Be sure to offer something sweet like fresh fruit or jam; something salty like pickles, olives, and cured meats; and something crunchy like nuts, crackers, or crostini. A balanced cheese selection is another must. Check out "Dress It Up With Cheese" (page 121) for ideas for choosing young, fresh cheeses, soft ripened cheeses, and dry-aged cheeses. Choose at least one from each category for a well-rounded selection.

Thanks to these vendors

We wish to thank the following vendors and resources whose products were photographed on the pages of this book.

Accent Décor

Accents de Ville

Arhaus

Blue Ocean Traders

Bobo Intriguing Objects

Crate & Barrel

Creative Co-op

Dogwood Hill

Ebay

Etsy

Factory Direct Craft

Fresh Market

Hobby Lobby

HomArt

Home Goods

Ivystone

June Home Supply

McGee & Co.

Michaels Stores

Overstock

Paper Lantern Store

Paper Source

Park Hill Collection

Pottery Barn

Target

Terrain

Trader Joe's

Tuesday Morning

Wayfair

West Elm

Woodland Hills Farms

Zazzle Inc.

Zodax

Special thanks to these small businesses, artisans, and restaurants:

A'mano

Ashley Mac's

At Home

Bloomstream Floral Design

Blueroot

Brick & Tin

Civil Stoneware

Davis Wholesale Florist

Dish'n It Out

Gilchrist

Hall's Birmingham Wholesale Florist

Leaf & Petal

Little Hardware

ME Home

Mountain Goat Market

Oak Street Garden Shop

Old Dairy Christmas Tree Farm

Table Matters

Wild Feather Farm (Etsy)

Thanks to these homeowners

The Montgomery Family

The Monfore Family

The Polmatier Family

The Ware Family

The Monteagle Sunday School Assembly community

General Index

Metric Charts

The recipes that appear in this cookbook use the standard US method for measuring liquid and dry or solid ingredients (teaspoons, tablespoons, and cups). The information on these pages is provided to help cooks outside the United States successfully use these recipes. All equivalents are approximate.

Metric Equivalents for Different Types of Ingredients

A standard cup measure of a dry or solid ingredient will vary in weight depending on the type of ingredient. A standard cup of liquid is the same volume for any type of liquid. Use the following chart when converting standard cup measures to grams (weight) or milliliters (volume).

STANDARD CUP	FINE POWDER (ex. flour)	GRAIN (ex. rice)	GRANULAR (ex. sugar)	LIQUID SOLIDS (ex. butter)	LIQUID (ex. milk)
1	140 g	150 g	190 g	200 g	240 ml
¾	105 g	113 g	143 g	150 g	180 ml
⅔	93 g	100 g	125 g	133 g	160 ml
½	70 g	75 g	95 g	100 g	120 ml
⅓	47 g	50 g	63 g	67 g	80 ml
¼	35 g	38 g	48 g	50 g	60 ml
⅛	18 g	19 g	24 g	25 g	30 ml

Useful Equivalents for Dry Ingredients by Weight

(To convert ounces to grams, multiply the number of ounces by 30.)

OZ	LB	G
1 oz	1/16 lb	30 g
4 oz	¼ lb	120 g
8 oz	½ lb	240 g
12 oz	¾ lb	360 g
16 oz	1 lb	480 g

Useful Equivalents for Length

(To convert inches to centimeters, multiply the number of inches by 2.5.)

IN	FT	YD	CM	M
1 in			2.5 cm	
6 in	½ ft		15 cm	
12 in	1 ft		30 cm	
36 in	3 ft	1 yd	90 cm	
40 in			100 cm	1 m

Useful Equivalents for Liquid Ingredients by Volume

TSP	TBSP	CUPS	FL OZ	ML	L
¼ tsp				1 ml	
½ tsp				2 ml	
1 tsp				5 ml	
3 tsp	1 Tbsp		½ fl oz	15 ml	
	2 Tbsp	⅛ cup	1 fl oz	30 ml	
	4 Tbsp	¼ cup	2 fl oz	60 ml	
	5⅓ Tbsp	⅓ cup	3 fl oz	80 ml	
	8 Tbsp	½ cup	4 fl oz	120 ml	
	10⅔ Tbsp	⅔ cup	5 fl oz	160 ml	
	12 Tbsp	¾ cup	6 fl oz	180 ml	
	16 Tbsp	1 cup	8 fl oz	240 ml	
	1 pt	2 cups	16 fl oz	480 ml	
	1 qt	4 cups	32 fl oz	960 ml	
			33 fl oz	1000 ml	1 l

Useful Equivalents for Cooking/Oven Temperatures

	FAHRENHEIT	CELSIUS	GAS MARK
FREEZE WATER	32° F	0° C	
ROOM TEMPERATURE	68° F	20° C	
BOIL WATER	212° F	100° C	
	325° F	160° C	3
	350° F	180° C	4
	375° F	190° C	5
	400° F	200° C	6
	425° F	220° C	7
	450° F	230° C	8
BROIL			Grill

Recipe Index

©2021 Southern Living Books, a division of Meredith Corporation
225 Liberty Street, New York, NY 10281

MEREDITH CONSUMER MARKETING
Director, Direct Marketing-Books: Daniel Fagan
Marketing Operations Manager: Max Daily
Assistant Marketing Manager: Kylie Dazzo
Content Manager: Julie Doll
Senior Production Manager: Liza Ward

PRODUCED BY
BLUELINE CREATIVE GROUP LLC
Visit: bluelinecreativegroup.com
Executive Producer/Editor: Katherine Cobbs
Art Director: Matt Ryan
Location Photographer: Becky Luigart-Stayner and Laurey Glenn
Location Stylists: Kay E. Clarke, Melanie Clarke, Katherine Cobbs, Sara Gae Waters, and Rebecca Withers
Copy Editor: Susan H. Ray

STUDIO PHOTOGRAPHY & RECIPES
MEREDITH FOOD STUDIOS
Director: Allison Lowery
Photography Director: Sheri Wilson
Studio Photographers: Antonis Achilleos, Jen Causey, and Greg Dupree
Studio Prop Stylist: Kay E. Clarke
Studio Food Stylist: Margaret Monroe Dickey, Rishon Hanners

PRINT PRODUCTION
WATERBURY PUBLICATIONS, INC.

Library of Congress Control Number: 2021932415

ISBN-13: 978-1-4197-5797-6

First Edition 2021
Printed in the United States of America
10 9 8 7 6 5 4 3 2 1
Call 1-800-826-4707 for more information

Distributed in 2021 by Abrams, an imprint of ABRAMS.
Abrams® is a registered trademark of Harry N. Abrams, Inc.

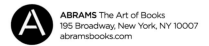

ABRAMS The Art of Books
195 Broadway, New York, NY 10007
abramsbooks.com

HOLIDAY PLANNER

Get ahead of the holiday frenzy with this helpful planner. Organize guest lists, jot down gifts for family and friends, and stay on top of every detail for a lovely low-stress holiday.

November 2021

SUNDAY	MONDAY	TUESDAY	WEDNESDAY
	Send Thanksgiving invites, plan menu (page 65), and create shopping list. **1**	Make a list to get the house guest-ready. Tackle repair and tidy up. **2**	Get in the holiday mood by lighting a gingerbread or pine candle. **3**
Daylight savings time ends. Turn clocks back for an extra hour of rest! **7**	Take inventory of pots, pan,s and baking dishes. Buy or borrow any needed. **8**	Plan a centerpiece and buy extra candles. **9**	Get holiday cards and start your list (page 189). **10**
Buy nonperishables in bulk to save on pricier items, like nuts and dried fruit. **14**	Start tidying the least-used rooms in the house, which are less likely to get messy again. **15**	Round up board games, playing cards, and photo albums to entertain guests while you're busy in the kitchen. **16**	Iron linens you plan to use and polish the silver. **17**
Serving a frozen turkey? Allow one day to thaw in the fridge for every 4 lbs. of bird. **21**	Create space in the coat closet and vacuum and dust the entry. **22**	Baking a pie? Be sure you've got what you need. **23**	Buy fresh flowers and other perishables needed and assemble centerpiece. **24**
Time to start thinking Christmas! **28**	If you prefer online shopping, start clicking! Cyber Monday is here. **29**	Gather recipes, plan Christmas menus (page 699), and clip coupons. **30**	

THURSDAY	FRIDAY	SATURDAY
Request gift ideas now so you can start holiday shopping early. **4**	Serving fresh turkey for Thanksgiving? Order now. **5**	Lay out serving pieces you plan to use. Attach sticky notes with what will go in each. **6**
Confirm headcount for Thanksgiving dinner. **11**	Need a kids' table? Cover a small table with kraft paper and provide crayons. **12**	Organize fridge and wipe shelves using 2 Tbsp. baking soda mixed with 1 qt. warm water. **13**
Make a prep list for each dish. Draw up a daily plan from now through Thanksgiving Day to spread tasks out. **18**	Shop for perishable grocery items such as milk, cheese and produce. **19**	Throwing a holiday cocktail party? Get invites out now. Calendars fill up fast! **20**
Happy Thanksgiving! Accept help from guests so you can relax and enjoy the day. **Thanksgiving 25**	Shoppers, start your engines— it's Black Friday! **26**	Enjoy those Thanksgiving leftovers. **27**

Holiday Hotlines

Use these toll-free numbers when you have last-minute food questions.

USDA Meat & Poultry Hotline:
1-888-674-6854

FDA Center for Food Safety:
1-888-723-3366

Butterball Turkey Talk-Line:
1-800-288-8372

Extra To-Dos

December 2021

SUNDAY	MONDAY	TUESDAY	WEDNESDAY
			Call the chimney sweep! **1**
Make cookie dough and freeze, or bake cookies and cakes and freeze unfrosted. **5**	Send out holiday cards. Don't wait until post office lines grow. **6**	Find volunteer opportunities. Donate food or gifts. Deliver a meal. **7**	Gather unused gift cards and check expirations. Use them to buy gifts for others. **8**
Make a gingerbread house! **12**	Wrap holiday gifts. **13**	Bake and decorate holiday cookies. **14**	Keep your Christmas tree fresh and hydrated. Replenish water pan daily. **15**
Take a break and treat yourself to a hot bath, coffee with a friend, or a nap. **19**	Watch "It's a Wonderful Life" by a roaring fire. **20**	It's the first day of winter and shortest day of the year—days will start getting longer now! **21**	Simmer cloves, allspice, an apple, and cinnamon stick in water to festively scent your home. **22**
Indulge in inventive leftovers from your holiday dinner (page 111). .... **Boxing Day 26**	Having a NYE Party? Beat the rush. Shop today. **27**	Phone loved ones you missed this holiday. **28**	Return or exchange any gifts before return deadlines. **29**

THURSDAY	FRIDAY	SATURDAY
Make a holiday playlist. **2**	Organize gift wrap, cards, ribbons, tape, and scissors. **3**	Get crafty. Plan homemade gifts and decorating projects. **4**
Make a natural garland of cranberries or popcorn using dental floss. **9**	Pull out, test, and string holiday lights; put them on a timer. **10**	Trim the tree, hang wreaths, display cards and dust off Christmas accents. The sooner you finish, the longer you can enjoy them. **11**
Acknowledge those who brighten your day—teacher, mail carrier, babysitter, favorite colleague—with a small gift. **16**	Finalize online purchases today before shipping prices jump. **17**	Bundle up and head out to enjoy the Christmas lights. **18**
Organize the stocking stuffers. **23**	Gather loved ones for a Cozy Winter Supper (page 89). **Christmas Eve 24**	Merry Christmas! Enjoy a Classic Christmas Feast (page 99). **Christmas 25**
Don't wait for resolutions, squeeze in a workout. **30**	Toast 2022 with friends and loved ones! **New Year's Eve 31**	

Extra To-Dos

Decorating Planner

Here's a list of details and finishing touches you can use to
tailor a picture-perfect house this holiday season.

Decorative materials needed

FROM THE YARD ....

FROM AROUND THE HOUSE ....

FROM THE STORE..

OTHER..

Holiday decorations

FOR THE TABLE ....

FOR THE DOOR..

FOR THE MANTEL...

FOR THE STAIRCASE ....

OTHER..

Create a Decorator's Toolkit

Our photo stylists guard their toolkits like the family jewels. A well-stocked kit means you have
just what you need at the ready to get you through the holidays and beyond.

- ☐ Tools (hammer, screwdrivers, clamps)
- ☐ Nails, screws, s-hooks, tacks
- ☐ Command strips and hooks
- ☐ Staple gun and staples
- ☐ Hot glue gun and glue sticks
- ☐ Craft glue
- ☐ Super Glue
- ☐ Clothespins
- ☐ Funnel
- ☐ Tape measure
- ☐ Twine

- ☐ Fishing line
- ☐ Green floral wire
- ☐ Sewing kit
- ☐ Lint roller
- ☐ Steamer or iron
- ☐ Paint brushes (assorted)
- ☐ Scissors
- ☐ Floral snips
- ☐ Lighter
- ☐ Batteries (assorted)
- ☐ Fuses for Christmas lights
- ☐ Scotch tape

- ☐ Double-stick tape
- ☐ Painters' tape
- ☐ Museum Wax
- ☐ Putty
- ☐ Goo Gone
- ☐ WD-40
- ☐ Window cleaner
- ☐ Furniture polish
- ☐ Touch-up paint
- ☐ Static duster
- ☐ Stain stick

Chestnuts 101

Because "chestnuts roasting" should be a thing again!

Order

Order whole chestnuts from a local grower or online no more than about 1 month before you plan to roast them.

Store

Store them in the refrigerator in a brown paper grocery bag until about 5 days before you plan to roast them. The paper bag is breathable so the chestnuts will stay moist and fresh. If stored in an airtight container they will mildew.

Cure

Fresh chestnuts are hard and bland if peeled and eaten without curing. To cure, remove the whole nuts from the refrigerator and leave them in a bowl away from direct sunlight at room temperature for 3 to 5 days. This will allow the starch in the nuts to convert to sugar. You will know that they are ready when they give slightly when pressed between finger and thumb.

Prepare

WARNING: Chestnut shells must be punctured or scored before cooking to release pressure, otherwise they can explode when cooking.

OVEN-ROASTING: Score the shell on the rounded side of each cured chestnut with an X. Arrange in a single layer on a baking sheet and sprinkle lightly with water. Bake at 425°F for 20 minutes, or until the outer shell curls away from the nut where it was scored. Peel the nuts while they are still warm.

FIRE-ROASTING: Score as above. Place the chestnuts in a dry cast iron skillet on a cooking grate set over hot coals or over indirect medium-high heat on a grill. Shake the skillet regularly to heat all sides of the nuts. Remove from the skillet when the shells have curled away where scored. Peel the nuts while they are warm.

BOILING CHESTNUTS: Halve the nuts with a sharp knife and boil them with enough water to cover for 10 to 15 minutes. Drain and remove the flesh from the shells while warm. Do not overcook or the flesh will be dry and mealy.

ENJOY the peeled nuts warm with salt and butter.

Party Planner

Stay on top of your party plans with this time-saving menu organizer.

GUESTS	WHAT THEY'RE BRINGING	SERVING PIECES NEEDED
....	☐ appetizer ☐ beverage ☐ bread ☐ main dish ☐ side dish ☐ dessert	....
....	☐ appetizer ☐ beverage ☐ bread ☐ main dish ☐ side dish ☐ dessert	....
....	☐ appetizer ☐ beverage ☐ bread ☐ main dish ☐ side dish ☐ dessert	....
....	☐ appetizer ☐ beverage ☐ bread ☐ main dish ☐ side dish ☐ dessert	....
....	☐ appetizer ☐ beverage ☐ bread ☐ main dish ☐ side dish ☐ dessert	....
....	☐ appetizer ☐ beverage ☐ bread ☐ main dish ☐ side dish ☐ dessert	....
....	☐ appetizer ☐ beverage ☐ bread ☐ main dish ☐ side dish ☐ dessert	....
....	☐ appetizer ☐ beverage ☐ bread ☐ main dish ☐ side dish ☐ dessert	....
....	☐ appetizer ☐ beverage ☐ bread ☐ main dish ☐ side dish ☐ dessert	....
....	☐ appetizer ☐ beverage ☐ bread ☐ main dish ☐ side dish ☐ dessert	....
....	☐ appetizer ☐ beverage ☐ bread ☐ main dish ☐ side dish ☐ dessert	....
....	☐ appetizer ☐ beverage ☐ bread ☐ main dish ☐ side dish ☐ dessert	....
....	☐ appetizer ☐ beverage ☐ bread ☐ main dish ☐ side dish ☐ dessert	....
....	☐ appetizer ☐ beverage ☐ bread ☐ main dish ☐ side dish ☐ dessert	....
....	☐ appetizer ☐ beverage ☐ bread ☐ main dish ☐ side dish ☐ dessert	....
....	☐ appetizer ☐ beverage ☐ bread ☐ main dish ☐ side dish ☐ dessert	....

Party Guest List

Party To-Do List

Christmas Dinner Planner

Use this space to create a menu, to-do list, and guest list for your special holiday celebration.

Menu Ideas

Dinner To-Do List

Christmas Dinner Guest List

Pantry List

Grocery List

Gifts & Greetings

Keep up with family's and friends' sizes, jot down gift ideas, and record purchases in this convenient chart. Also, use it to keep track of addresses for your Christmas card list.

Gift List and Size Charts

GIFT PURCHASED/MADE   SENT

....

jeans____ shirt____ sweater____ jacket____ shoes____ belt____
blouse____ skirt____ slacks____ dress____ suit____ coat____
pajamas____ robe____ hat____ gloves____ ring____

jeans____ shirt____ sweater____ jacket____ shoes____ belt____
blouse____ skirt____ slacks____ dress____ suit____ coat____
pajamas____ robe____ hat____ gloves____ ring____

jeans____ shirt____ sweater____ jacket____ shoes____ belt____
blouse____ skirt____ slacks____ dress____ suit____ coat____
pajamas____ robe____ hat____ gloves____ ring____

jeans____ shirt____ sweater____ jacket____ shoes____ belt____
blouse____ skirt____ slacks____ dress____ suit____ coat____
pajamas____ robe____ hat____ gloves____ ring____

jeans____ shirt____ sweater____ jacket____ shoes____ belt____
blouse____ skirt____ slacks____ dress____ suit____ coat____
pajamas____ robe____ hat____ gloves____ ring____

jeans____ shirt____ sweater____ jacket____ shoes____ belt____
blouse____ skirt____ slacks____ dress____ suit____ coat____
pajamas____ robe____ hat____ gloves____ ring____

jeans____ shirt____ sweater____ jacket____ shoes____ belt____
blouse____ skirt____ slacks____ dress____ suit____ coat____
pajamas____ robe____ hat____ gloves____ ring____

Christmas Card List

NAME	ADDRESS	SENT

Holiday Memories

Hold on to priceless Christmas memories forever with handwritten recollections of this season's magical moments.

Treasured Traditions

Keep track of your family's favorite holiday customs and pastimes on these lines.

Special Holiday Activities

What holiday events do you look forward to year after year? Write them down here.

Holiday Visits and Visitors

Keep a list of this year's holiday visitors.
Jot down friend and family news as well.

....
....
....
....
....
....
....
....
....
....
....
....
....
....
....
....
....
....
....
....
....
....
....

This Year's Favorite Recipes

APPETIZERS AND BEVERAGES ....
....
....
....
....

ENTRÉES ....
....
....
....

SIDES AND SALADS ....
....
....
....

COOKIES AND CANDIES ....
....
....
....

DESSERTS ....
....
....
....

Looking Ahead

Holiday Wrap-up

Use this checklist to record thank-you notes sent for holiday gifts and hospitality.

NAME	GIFT AND/OR EVENT	NOTE SENT
....	....	☐
....	....	☐
....	....	☐
....	....	☐
....	....	☐
....	....	☐
....	....	☐
....	....	☐
....	....	☐
....	....	☐
....	....	☐
....	....	☐
....	....	☐

Notes for Next Year

Write down your ideas for Christmas 2022 on the lines below.

....

....

....

....

....

....

....

....

....

....

....